A CHANCE TO SET
THE RECORD STRAIGHT

A. J. Foyt, Mark Spitz, Jim Brown, Bart Starr, Johnny Unitas, Sandy Koufax, Ted Williams, Yogi Berra, Lou Brock, Archie Moore, Oscar Robertson, Bobby Orr, Bobby Jones, Jerry West, Gordie Howe, Chi Cheng, Wilt Chamberlain, Lee Trevino, Rod Laver . . .

Smashers all, what they and the hundreds of other superstars have in common here in THE ILLUSTRATED SPORTS RECORD BOOK is, of course, a record (or several). Covering an array of sports, their history-making marks have set a standard for athletes to shoot at—and for you to use as a guide when watching your favorite sport.

SIGNET Books You'll Enjoy

THE ILLUSTRATED SPORTS RECORD BOOK

*by Zander Hollander
and David Schulz*

AN ASSOCIATED FEATURES BOOK

SIGNET

NEW AMERICAN LIBRARY

TIMES MIRROR

ACKNOWLEDGMENTS

All the photographs in this book are used with the permission of United Press International, Inc., save for the following:
Herb Weitman, page 20; Rod Hanna, page 22; Malcolm W. Emmons,
page 23; Malcolm W. Emmons, page 29; Cincinnati Bengals, page 38;
Carl Skalak, Jr., page 111; Carl Skalak, Jr., page 112; Malcolm W. Emmons, page 122; San Francisco Examiner, page 124; Malcolm W. Emmons, page 125; Darryl Norenberg, page 133; Philadelphia 76ers, page
134; Malcolm W. Emmons, page 138; The San Diego Union, page 139;
Hall of Fame, page 142; Scotty Kilpatrick, page 144; Hall of Fame,
page 145; Dick Raphael, page 148; Robert B. Shaver, page 150; Frank
Bryan, page 153.

CONTENTS

BASEBALL

PRO BASKETBALL

HOCKEY

COLLEGE FOOTBALL

COLLEGE BASKETBALL

TRACK AND FIELD

GOLF

TENNIS

BOXING

AUTO RACING

SWIMMING

HORSE RACING

INTRODUCTION

Records, they say, are made to be broken, and usually they are. "Hoss" Radbourne, wherever he is, will object to this thesis and will stand—well, not without support—on the record. "Hoss," a pitcher for the National League's Providence team, won 60 games in a single season. That was in 1884, and the record stands.

It is a somewhat safer mark than, say, Wilt Chamberlain's 100 points (and Frank Selvy's 100) in a basketball game, George Blanda's 68 pass attempts in a football game, Hugh Duffy's .438 batting average, Phil Esposito's 76 goals and 152 points in a single hockey season, UCLA's 88-game winning streak in basketball, Bobby Jones' golfing grand slam, Rod Laver's pair of tennis grand slams, and Mark Spitz' seven Olympic gold medals in swimming.

The aforementioned are among the 350 records and nearly 200 stories covered in *The Illustrated Sports Record Book*. The goal here was to record these various feats as they might have appeared in a newspaper at the time of achievement.

The presence of so many nostalgic names in this collection is significant. Certainly superstars set super marks, but it is intriguing to note how many of the records set in yesteryear have stood the test of modern assault by the new breed.

Thus it is that this unique army of achievers has Bill Russell and Bob Pettit to go with Jerry West and Nate Archibald; Glenn Davis and Doc Blanchard with Virgil Carter and Jim Plunkett; Babe Ruth, Ty Cobb, Carl Hubbell, and Joe DiMaggio with Willie Mays, Hank Aaron, and Lou Brock; Sammy Baugh, Don Hutson, Jim Brown, and Gale Sayers with Joe Namath, Bart Starr, Johnny Unitas, and O.J. Simpson; Rocket Richard, Ted Lindsay, and Gordie Howe with Tony Esposito and Bobby Orr; Bobby Jones and Ben Hogan with Jack Nicklaus, Mickey Wright, and Lee Trevino; Helen Wills Moody with Rod Laver.

They are only a partial lineup of a cast of hundreds whose records were alive and well as this book went to press.

PRO FOOTBALL

Nevers-Nevers Land

CHICAGO, Illinois, November 28, 1929—The holiday air permeated snow-covered Comiskey Park today as a Thanksgiving Day crowd of 8,000 watched the Bears and Cardinals battle for the championship of Chicago. Earlier, the two teams had played a scoreless tie, and with losing records neither was headed for a championship of anything but the Windy City.

An injured Red Grange said he was ready to play for the Bears, and an overweight, overage Jim Thorpe came out of retirement again to put in a token appearance with the Cardinals and add to the holiday festivities. Thorpe wasn't going to be much help to the South Siders, but the Cards were counting on powerful Ernie Nevers, the product of Superior, Wisconsin, who went to Stanford and almost single-handedly took on Notre Dame's Four Horsemen in the 1926 Rose Bowl.

Nevers scored the second time the Cards had the ball, going 20 yards in the swirling snow behind a block by Duke Slater. Before the first half was over, Nevers scored twice more and booted a pair of extra points to give the Cardinals a 20-0 halftime lead.

The second half was almost a carbon copy of the first, with Nevers scoring three more touchdowns and kicking two points after. The Bears tallied on a 60-yard pass from Walt Homer to Garland Grange, Red's brother. Nevers' six touchdowns established an NFL record, as did his total of 40 points.

Most points scored, game: 40, Ernie Nevers, Chicago Cardinals, vs. Chicago Bears, November 28, 1929 (6 touchdowns, 4 PATs)

Hutson's Haul

BOSTON, Massachusetts, November 18, 1945—The Alabama Antelope, Don Hutson, came off the bench today to catch five of the eight passes thrown his way, score a touchdown, gain six yards rushing, and kick four extra points in the Green Bay Packers' 28-0 triumph over the Boston Yanks before a crowd of more than 30,000 in Fenway Park.

The 6-foot 1-inch, 190-pound Hutson, who played in the 1935 Rose Bowl when Dixie Howell was the 'Bama quarterback, has been doing more place-kicking than pass-catching this season, his eleventh as a pro. But Hutson was catching them today, and the

Green Bay's Don Hutson caught a record 99 touchdown passes.

10-yard scoring pitch from Irv Comp in the second quarter extended his record total of touchdown receptions to 99.

Hutson, who has led the NFL in scoring five times, is the only player ever to be honored twice as MVP—he was singled out in 1941 and again in 1942 as the NFL's top player.

Most touchdowns on pass receptions, career: 99, Don Hutson, Green Bay Packers, 1935-45

Ram Catcher

DETROIT, Michigan, November 22, 1945–Don Hutson move over, Jim Benton has arrived. The 6-foot 3-inch, 210-pound Ben-

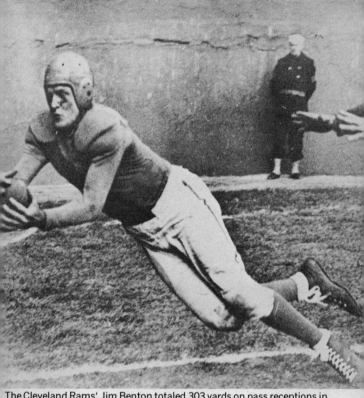

The Cleveland Rams' Jim Benton totaled 303 yards on pass receptions in one game.

ton was on the receiving end of 10 Bob Waterfield passes today as the Cleveland Rams sewed up the NFL's Western Division championship with a 28–21 decision over the Detroit Lions.

Benton, who scored two touchdowns and set up a third with his receptions, accounted for 303 yards, breaking the mark of 237 yards set by the Green Bay veteran, Don Hutson, two years ago. Waterfield completed only two other passes all day, for 26 yards, as more than 40,000 chilled Lion fans watched in Briggs Stadium.

Most yardage on pass receptions, game: 303 yards, Jim Benton, Cleveland Rams, vs. Detroit Lions, November 22, 1945

Slingin' Sammy

WASHINGTON, D.C., December 9, 1945—Slingin' Sammy Baugh led the Washington Redskins to a fifth NFL Eastern Division championship as the Redskins completed 11 of 20 passes today on the way to a 17–0 victory over the New York Giants.

The 6-foot 2-inch, 180-pound Baugh finished the season with 128 completions in 182 attempts for an eye-popping 70.3 percent passing efficiency as he guided Washington to an 8 and 2 won-lost record from the modern "T" formation.

When Baugh came into the professional ranks from Texas Christian University, the Redskins were using the single-wing formation on offense. In recent years they added more and more plays from the "T," and this season the transformation was complete.

In addition to the five divisional titles, Baugh has led Washington to league championships in 1937, his rookie year; 1940, and 1943.

Highest passing efficiency, season: 70.3 percent, Sammy Baugh, Washington Redskins, 1945 (128 of 182)

Washington's Sammy Baugh completed 70.3 percent of his passes in 1945.

Long-Range Gage

CHICAGO, Illinois, December 4, 1949—The Pittsburgh Steelers finally scored more than one touchdown against the Chicago Bears, but they still lost, 30–21.

Bob Gage, a fleet-footed rookie out of Clemson, dashed 97 yards early in the fourth quarter to score the Steelers' second touchdown of the day. It was the first time since these two teams began meeting in 1934 that Pittsburgh scored more than a single TD against the Bears. Gage's long run from scrimmage matched the league record set by Green Bay's Andy Uram a decade ago.

Only 44 seconds after his long run, Gage was called on again. The Steelers had recovered a Bear fumble and Gage carried six yards for another touchdown. But the running of Julie Rykovich, the passing of Johnny Lujack, and the kicking of rookie George Blanda were more than enough to give the Bears the victory.

Longest run from scrimmage: 97 yards, Bob Gage, Pittsburgh Steelers, vs. Chicago Bears, December 4, 1949 (Ties Andy Uram, Green Bay Packers, vs. Chicago Cardinals, October 8, 1939)

Shaw 'Nuff

CHICAGO, Illinois, October 2, 1950—Baseball's regular season was barely concluded when the Chicago Cardinals swooped into Comiskey Park with a record-breaking aerial show on this crisp Monday evening.

Bringing their NFL record to one win, one loss, the Cardinals benefited from a precedent-setting pass-catching performance by Bob Shaw, a refugee from the All-America Football Conference. With Jim Hardy doing the throwing, Shaw was on the receiving end of five touchdown passes in the Cardinals' 55–13 romp over the Baltimore Colts.

The five TD receptions by Shaw, who played his college ball at Ohio State, broke the single-game mark of four shared by Don Hutson of Green Bay and Joe Carter of Philadelphia.

Hardy, who also threw a scoring pass to Evan Polafoot, fell one short of the touchdown-pass record of seven set by the Bears' Sid

Luckman in 1943. The other two Cardinal touchdowns tonight were scored by Charley Trippi on runs of 1 and 18 yards.

Most touchdowns on pass receptions, game: 5, Bob Shaw, Chicago Cardinals, vs. Baltimore Colts, October 2, 1950

Groundless Fears

LOS ANGELES, California, December 3, 1950—Led by the pass-catching of Tom Fears, the Los Angeles Rams went on a record-setting binge today in beating the Green Bay Packers, 51–14, to clinch at least a tie for the championship of the NFL's National Conference.

As the Rams were establishing seasonal records in 10 team offensive categories, the 6-foot 2-inch, 215-pound Fears was catching a record 18 passes to establish a single-game mark. The old league record of 14 receptions was set in 1940 by Don Looney of Philadelphia, and tied by Green Bay's Don Hutson in 1942, the Chicago Bears' Jimmy Keane in 1949, and the New York Bulldogs' Ralph Heywood, also last season.

With Norm Van Brocklin and Bob Waterfield passing, receivers like Fears and Elroy Hirsch, and runners like Glenn Davis and Tank Younger, the Rams have been an explosive offensive team all season. Just two weeks ago, against the New York Yanks, the Rams gained 636 yards, while the Yanks were picking up 497 yards to establish a record for most yards gained by two teams in one game: 1,133.

Most receptions, game: 18, Tom Fears, Los Angeles Rams, vs. Green Bay Packers, December 3, 1950
Most yards gained, both teams, game: 1,133, Los Angeles Rams (636) and New York Yanks (497), November 19, 1950

The Flingin' Dutchman

LOS ANGELES, California, September 28, 1951—Young Norm Van Brocklin made Ram fans forget about the injured Bob Waterfield and Glenn Davis today as he passed for 554 yards in leading Los Angeles past the New York Yanks, 54–14.

Los Angeles' Norm Van Brocklin passed for 554 yards against the New York Yankees.

Van Brocklin, who played college ball at Oregon, bettered the efforts of Chicago Bear quarterback Johnny Lujack, who passed for 468 yards two years ago.

Playing before a Friday night crowd of 30,315, Van Brocklin threw five touchdown aerials, four of them to Elroy "Crazylegs" Hirsch. The Rams' 34 first downs and 735 total yards also established league marks.

Most yardage, passing, game: 554, Norm Van Brocklin, Los Angeles Rams, vs. New York Yanks, September 28, 1951
Most yards gained, game, one team: 735, Los Angeles Rams, vs. New York Yanks, September 28, 1951

On the Right Track

LOS ANGELES, California, December 14, 1952—Dick "Night Train" Lane put the Los Angeles Rams into a playoff with the Detroit Lions today, but he won't be there to enjoy the fruits of his labor.

Lane intercepted three passes and ran back one for a touchdown to spark the defending champion Rams to their eighth straight victory, a 28–14 decision over Pittsburgh. The three interceptions gave Lane a record total of 14 for the season, surpassing the mark of 12 shared by Don Sandifer of Washington and Spec Sanders of the old New York Yankees.

A crowd of more than 70,000 was on hand to see Norm Van Brocklin throw a touchdown pass to Elroy Hirsch and two to Tom Fears as Bob Waterfield, in his last game for the Rams, was relegated to kicking extra points.

Pittsburgh quarterback Jim Finks was victimized four times by the Ram defense, and it was the last interception that brought Lane the record and put him out of the playoff game. Lane, a product of Scottsbluff, Nebraska, Junior College, and a former aircraft plant worker, was brought down hard after the interception, wrenching his knee and severely spraining his ankle.

Most interceptions, season: 14, Dick "Night Train" Lane, Los Angeles Rams, 1952

Dick "Night Train" Lane holds the NFL record with 14 interceptions in one game.

Green Bay's Paul Hornung scores touchdown against Los Angeles in the last game of his 176-point season.

Golden Boy

LOS ANGELES, California, December 17, 1960—Paul Hornung scored a fourth-quarter touchdown and followed that with his fifth extra point of the day to lead the Green Bay Packers past the Los Angeles Rams, 35–21, and on to their first divisional championship in 16 years.

Hornung, called "the Golden Boy" because of his golden locks and ability to come up with the "money play," scored on a one-yard plunge. The score, and extra points, brought his season's point total to a record 176. Hornung, who won the Heisman Trophy four years ago as a quarterback at Notre Dame, had broken the old scoring record of 138 points two weeks ago when he scored 23 points against the Chicago Bears. The record that Hornung broke had been set by Don Hutson in 1942. Hutson, incidentally, was on that last Packer team to win a divisional title, in 1944.

Most points, season: 176, Paul Hornung, Green Bay Packers, 1960 (15 touchdowns, 41 PATs, 15 field goals)

Return of the Century

DALLAS, Texas, October 15, 1961—The largest crowd in the Dallas Cowboys' two years of existence was on hand in the Cotton Bowl today. The 42,500 didn't see a Cowboy upset—the New York Giants won their fourth straight game, 31–10—but they saw an NFL record tied.

The mark came in the third quarter when Giant defensive back Erich Barnes picked off an Eddie LeBaron pass two yards deep in the end zone and sprinted down the field for a touchdown. The 102-yard return of an intercepted pass by Barnes, who played at Purdue, equaled the effort of Detroit's Bob Smith against the Chicago Bears in 1949.

Longest return of an intercepted pass: 102 yards, Erich Barnes, New York Giants, vs. Dallas Cowboys, October 15, 1961 (Ties Bob Smith, Detroit Lions, vs. Chicago Bears, November 24, 1949)

The New York Giants' Erich Barnes equaled the NFL standard with a 102-yard return of a pass interception.

11

Blanda to Whom?

SAN FRANCISCO, California, December 17, 1961—The big names in the Houston attack were on display today as George Blanda, Billy Cannon, Charlie Tolar, and Willard Dewveall accounted for most of the points as the Oilers clinched the AFL's Eastern Division championship with a 47–16 rout of Oakland. Instead of one of the big names, however, it will be Bill Groman's name that will go into the record book.

Playing in muddy Candlestick Park before a slim crowd of 4,821, Blanda threw four touchdown passes, including one to Groman. Groman, who usually replaces Dewveall or flanker Charlie Hennigan after the game has started, is not among the leading receivers in the league, but his touchdown catch was his seventeenth of the season, equaling the single-season total of Don Hutson with the Green Bay Packers and Elroy Hirsch with the Los Angeles Rams.

The Blanda-to-Groman pass from the 7-yard line came in the second quarter when the Oilers were leading by just three points, 12–9. It was Blanda's second TD strike of the day. His two others gave him a season's total of 36.

Most touchdown receptions, season: 17, Bill Groman, Houston Oilers, 1961 (Ties Don Hutson, Green Bay Packers, 1942; Elroy Hirsch, Los Angeles Rams, 1951)

Taylor Made

LOS ANGELES, California, December 16, 1962—Sparked by Jimmy Taylor's running and his record nineteenth touchdown of the season, the Green Bay Packers took the NFL Western Division championship with a 20–17 victory over the Los Angeles Rams.

This game was much more important when it started than when it ended, since the Packers thought they had to win it to clinch the championship. Instead, they had the crown anyway, since the Chicago Bears upset the Detroit Lions earlier in the day.

Taylor rushed for 156 yards against the Rams, boosting his season's total to 1,574 yards. His touchdown, on a 28-yard burst in the second quarter, gives him the NFL record for most touchdowns by rushing in a season, since all 19 he scored were on the ground.

Most touchdowns rushing, season: 19, Jimmy Taylor, Green Bay Packers, 1962

Green Bay's Jimmy Taylor rushed for a record nineteenth touchdown against Los Angeles.

13

Houston's George Blanda attempted and completed more passes in one game than anyone else in pro football.

Cranked-Up Oiler

BUFFALO, New York, November 1, 1964—Houston's 37-year-old quarterback, George Blanda, established a pair of passing records today, but the Buffalo Bills scored 17 points in the final period to win, 24–10, and remain undefeated in eight American Football League games.

Blanda attempted a record 68 passes and completed 37, also a record; it wasn't enough to keep the Oilers from losing their fifth straight game. Blanda passed for 393 yards and Houston's only touchdown, an 11-yard strike to Willard Dewveall. But the Bills' running back tandem of Cookie Gilchrist and Bob Smith proved too strong for the Houston defense.

Most passes attempted, game: 68, George Blanda, Houston Oilers, vs. Buffalo Bills, November 1, 1964
Most passes completed, game: 37, George Blanda, Houston Oilers, vs. Buffalo Bills, November 1, 1964

Hennigan's Hundred and One

HOUSTON, Texas, December 20, 1964—As pass-master Sammy Baugh watched from the sidelines in his last game as head coach at the last Oiler game in Jeppesen Stadium, a pair of his Houston charges were passing their way into the record book today.

Wide receiver Charlie Hennigan, out of Northwest Louisiana, hauled in eight passes from George Blanda to give him 101 receptions for the season, breaking Lionel Taylor's AFL record by one, set with Denver in 1961. Hennigan's total also surpassed the NFL record 93 catches made by the Chicago Bears' Johnny Morris this season.

With Blanda's pinpoint accuracy—including a 25-yard scoring strike to Hennigan—the Oilers opened up a 24–0 lead in the first half and went on to a 34–15 triumph over Denver for only their fourth triumph in 14 games this season. For Blanda, who hit 16 of 27 passes today, he finished the year with 505 attempts and 262 completions, both better than the AFL marks of Denver's Frank Tripucka.

Most passes caught, season: 101, Charlie Hennigan, Houston Oilers, 1964

Running Wild

CHICAGO, Illinois, December 12, 1965—With the NFL's Western Division championship at stake, Chicago's Gale Sayers went on a scoring binge today in tying a 36-year-old record with a six-touchdown performance against the San Francisco 49ers. Winning today, 61–20, kept the Bears in contention with the Baltimore Colts and Green Bay Packers. (In Baltimore, Green Bay's Paul Hornung scored five TDs today in a 42–27 Packer triumph.)

The 6-foot, 200-pound Sayers, a rookie out of Kansas University, opened the scoring after gathering in a screen pass from Rudy Bukich. The play covered 80 yards, all of it on Sayers' running. The soft-spoken halfback then scored on runs of 21, 7, 50, and 1 yard before returning a punt 85 yards for his sixth touchdown, matching the number scored by Ernie Nevers of the Chicago Cardinals against the Bears on Thanksgiving Day, 1929, and Dub Jones of Cleveland, also against the Bears, in 1951.

Chicago Bears' Gale Sayers scores one of his six touchdowns against San Francisco.

After the game, Sayers was awarded the game ball and thus became the first player in Bear history to be awarded two game balls in one season. In addition to his TDs, Sayers picked up 113 yards rushing, 89 yards on pass receptions, and 134 yards on punt returns.

Most touchdowns, game: 6, Gale Sayers, Chicago Bears, vs. San Francisco 49ers, December 12, 1965 (Ties Ernie Nevers, Chicago Cardinals, vs. Chicago Bears, November 28, 1929; William "Dub" Jones, Cleveland Browns, vs. Chicago Bears, November 25, 1951)

Strung Out

CHICAGO, Illinois, December 12, 1965—Not that it made any difference in the final outcome, but for the first time in 235 attempts, San Francisco placekicker Tommy Davis missed an extra point today. The Chicago Bears were ahead, 20–7, when John David Crow scored on a 15-yard pass from John Brodie to make the score 20–13. Davis, a seven-year pro out of Louisiana State, missed the point after touchdown attempt. It was the first extra point he had missed since he began playing in the NFL in 1959.

The Bears, in the friendly confines of Wrigley Field and cheered by a crowd of 46,278, went on a scoring rampage, winning 61–20.

Most consecutive extra points: 234, Tommy Davis, San Francisco 49ers, September 27, 1959, to December 12, 1965.

Doing It Up Brown

ST. LOUIS, Missouri, December 19, 1965—The Cleveland Browns' Jim Brown, as stormy in temperament as he is talented in football, saw most of his last regular-season game from the bench today. Big No.32 was ejected from the game in the first half after fighting with the Cardinals' Joe Robb.

Before he left the game, though, the 6-foot 3-inch, 230-pound Brown gained 74 yards in 11 carries, scored his twenty-first touchdown of the season, and wound up with a battery of career records. His touchdown contributed to Cleveland's 27–24 victory

Cleveland's Jim Brown scores the last touchdown of his career against the St. Louis Cardinals.

over St. Louis that gave the Browns the best record in the NFL with 11 wins and 3 losses.

Among the many records of Brown, who never missed a game in his nine-year career, are:

Most yards rushing, career: 12,312, Jim Brown, Cleveland Browns, 1957–65

Most rushing attempts, career: 2,359, Jim Brown, Cleveland Browns, 1957–65

Most touchdowns, career: 126, Jim Brown, Cleveland Browns, 1957–65

Most touchdowns rushing, career: 106, Jim Brown, Cleveland Browns, 1957–65

Highest rushing average, career: 5.22 yards per carry, Jim Brown, Cleveland Browns, 1957–65

Most seasons leading league in rushing: 8, Jim Brown, Cleveland Browns, 1957–61, 1963–65

Most games, 100 or more yards rushing: 58, Jim Brown, Cleveland Browns, 1957–65

Gale Force

CHICAGO, Illinois, December 19, 1965—Gale Sayers, who scored six touchdowns in last week's game against the 49ers, scored another TD for the Bears today to give him a season record total of 22 as Chicago dropped a 24–17 decision to the Minnesota Vikings.

The brilliant running back from Omaha, Nebraska, by way of Kansas University, scored on a 2-yard plunge in the fourth quarter to give the Bears a 14–3 lead. The Bears, though, were playing listlessly after being eliminated from championship contention by virtue of a Baltimore victory over Los Angeles yesterday. Minnesota won the game when Rip Hawkins intercepted a Rudy Bukich pass and went 35 yards for a score late in the game.

Sayers, a rookie, had broken Lenny Moore's single-season record of 20 touchdowns with his splurge of six a week ago. Today's TD kept Sayers one ahead of Cleveland's Jim Brown, who scored his twenty-first of the season.

Most touchdowns, season: 22, Gale Sayers, Chicago Bears, 1965

Just for Kicks

PITTSBURGH, Pennsylvania, September 24, 1967—Jim Bakken has nothing to kick about now. The former reserve quarterback from the University of Wisconsin and full-time kicking specialist for the St. Louis Cardinals booted a record seven field goals as St. Louis beat Pittsburgh, 28–14, today.

In addition to making kicks of 18, 24, 33, 29, 24, 32, and 23 yards today, Bakken missed two attempts, from 45 and 50 yards away. The nine attempts are also an NFL record.

Garo Yepremian, last season, had converted on six of eight field goal tries for the Detroit Lions, but after kicking a field goal in his thirteenth successive game today, Jim Bakken had nothing else to kick about, since he owned the record. Cardinal defensive back Larry Wilson did though, for his part in Bakken's record went largely unnoticed. "Don't I get any credit for holding the ball?" Wilson asked after the game.

Most field goals attempted, game: 9, Jim Bakken, St. Louis Cardinals, vs. Pittsburgh Steelers, September 24, 1967
Most field goals, game: 7, Jim Bakken, St. Louis Cardinals, vs. Pittsburgh Steelers, September 24, 1967

St. Louis Cardinal Jim Bakken kicked seven field goals against the Pittsburgh Steelers.

Sonny at the Pass

WASHINGTON, D.C., December 17, 1967—Billy Kilmer led the New Orleans Saints to a 30–14 upset of the Washington Redskins today, but the visitors from the Land of the Mardi Gras could do nothing to stop Sonny Jurgensen from ending the season on a record-breaking note.

Washington's Sonny Jurgensen attempted and completed more passes in one season than any other quarterback.

With the Redskins never able to move ahead in the scoring during the course of the game, Jurgensen was forced to pass and pass and pass. The paunchy redhead threw the ball 49 times, completing 26. These gave him season totals of 508 attempts, 288 completions, both record numbers as Washington finished with a 5-6-3 record behind Dallas and Philadelphia in the NFL's four-team Capitol Division.

Most passes attempted, season: 508, Christian Adolph "Sonny" Jurgensen, Washington Redskins, 1967
Most passes completed, season: 288, Christian Adolph "Sonny" Jurgensen, Washington Redskins, 1967

Mr. Smith Returns

DENVER, Colorado, December 17, 1967—Diminutive Noland Smith scampered 106 yards with a kickoff today, equaling a pro record and helping the Kansas City Chiefs to a 38-24 victory over Denver in an American Football League game.

The jaunt by the 5-foot 8-inch, 160-pound Smith came in the third quarter after Len Dawson and Otis Taylor hooked up on

Kansas City's Noland Smith returned a kickoff 106 yards against Denver.

three scoring passes to boost the Chiefs to a 28–17 lead. Smith's runback—which equals the NFL mark established in 1956 by Green Bay's Al Carmichael against the Bears—came after Bob Humphreys had kicked an 18-yard field goal for the Broncos.

The victory, which gave Kansas City a 9–5 slate for the year, also saw the Chiefs' Mike Garrett reach the 1,000-yard rushing plateau this season and Jan Stenerud kick an AFL record twenty-first field goal this season.

Longest return of kickoff: 106 yards, Noland Smith, Kansas City Chiefs, vs. Denver Broncos, December 17, 1967 (Ties Al Carmichael, Green Bay Packers, vs. Chicago Bears, October 7, 1956)

Class by Himself

SAN DIEGO, California, December 24, 1967—Joe Namath has often done things no other football player has, and today he plowed more virgin territory, passing a football for more than

Joe Namath of the New York Jets is the only man to pass for more than 4,000 yards in one season.

4,000 yards in a single pro football season.

The round-shouldered glamour boy of the New York Jets led his team to a 42–31 victory over the San Diego Chargers by completing 18 of 26 passes for 343 yards and four touchdowns. Namath played the game wearing a special mask to protect a broken jaw. The 343 yards passing raised his season's total to 4,007 yards, bettering the 3,746 achieved by Washington's Sonny Jurgensen in the NFL season-closer last week.

Namath's efforts today brought a halt to the Jets' three-game losing streak, raising the season's record to 8 victories, 5 losses, and a tie, the first winning season in the history of the New York franchise in the AFL. In addition, the Jets finished in second place, only a game behind the Houston Oilers in the AFL Eastern Division.

Most yards gained passing, season: 4,007, Joe Namath, New York Jets, 1967

Washington's Sonny Jurgensen completed a 99-yard pass play to Gerry Allen in this game against the Chicago Bears.

99 or Bust

CHICAGO, Illinois, September 15, 1968—Christian Adolph Jurgensen threw his way into the record book today, not with his four touchdown passes, nor by leading the Washington Redskins to a 38–28 upset of the Chicago Bears in today's season opener.

The former Duke quarterback, who set a record for most passes and most completions in last season's final game, started this new season on a throwing note, despite having undergone elbow surgery in the off-season. Jurgensen teamed with tight end Gerry Allen on a 99-yard pass play, equaling the longest touchdown bomb in NFL history.

The record came in the second quarter after the Bears had narrowed the Redskin lead to seven points, 14–7. Brig Owens had stopped a Chicago threat with an interception on the 1-yard line. It was then that Jurgensen, standing deep in his own end zone, spotted Allen open on the 31-yard line, drilled the ball to him, and watched the converted running back out of Omaha carry the ball

69 more yards to paydirt, duplicating the feat of three other receivers.

Most yards on a completed pass: 99, Christian Adolph "Sonny" Jurgensen to Gerry Allen, Washington Redskins, vs. Chicago Bears, September 15, 1968 (Ties Frank Filchock to Andy Farkas, Washington Redskins, vs. Pittsburgh Steelers, October 15, 1939; George Izo to Bobby Mitchell, Washington Redskins, vs. Cleveland Browns, September 15, 1963; Karl Sweetan to Pat Studstill, Detroit Lions, vs. Baltimore Colts, October 16, 1966)

Jet Kicks

MIAMI, Florida, December 15, 1968—The crippled New York Jets, with an eye toward playing in the Super Bowl here next month, prepared for the AFL championship game with Kansas

New York Jet Jim Turner holds the pro record of 34 field goals in a season.

City next week by outclassing the three-year-old expansion Miami Dolphins, 31–7.

Receiver Don Maynard and linemen Bob Talamini and Dave Herman saw little or no action for the Jets, while running back Emerson Boozer played for the first time in three weeks.

On the positive side, Joe Namath, playing half a game, completed six of ten passes for 120 yards and Jim Turner booted his longest field goal of the year. Turner's 49-yarder in the first quarter was his thirty-fourth of the season, a professional record.

Most field goals, season: 34, Jim Turner, New York Jets, 1968

Kapp-ital Performance

BLOOMINGTON, Minnesota, September 28, 1969—Most sports fans' minds were on baseball today as the Atlanta Braves clinched the National League's Western Division pennant to join the New York Mets, Minnesota Twins, and Baltimore Orioles in baseball's new-fangled intra-league playoffs that were instituted this season.

But Chicano Joe Kapp and the Minnesota Vikings put on a record-breaking performance that made folks in Metropolitan Stadium here forget about the summer sport. Kapp, the University of California quarterback who played in Canada before becoming a Viking, hit six different receivers with seven touchdown passes, equaling the passing performances of Sid Luckman in 1943, Y.A. Tittle in 1962, George Blanda in 1961, and Adrian Burk in 1954. Burk, who played for the Philadelphia Eagles, was on the field today, working the game as a back judge.

With Vice President Spiro Agnew—former governor of Maryland—in the stands to root for the defending champion Baltimore Colts, Kapp hit Gene Washington twice and Dave Osborn, Bob Grim, Kent Kramer, John Beasley, and Jim Lindsey once each to lead Minnesota past Baltimore, 52–14. Overall, Kapp connected with 12 different receivers in passing for 449 yards before a sellout crowd of 47,644.

Most touchdown passes thrown, game: 7, Joe Kapp, Minnesota Vikings, vs. Baltimore Colts, September 28, 1969 (Ties Sid Luckman, Chicago Bears, vs. New York Giants, November 14, 1943; Adrian Burk, Philadelphia Eagles, vs. Washington Redskins, October 17, 1954; George Blanda, Houston Oilers, vs. New York Titans, November 19, 1961; Y. A. Tittle, New York Giants, vs. Washington Redskins, October 28, 1962)

Minnesota's Joe Kapp passed for seven touchdowns against the Colts.

New Orleans' Tom Dempsey boots a 63-yard field goal against Detroit.

Prodigious Boot

NEW ORLEANS, Louisiana, November 8, 1970—Trailing 17–16 with two seconds left to play and the ball on their own 45-yard line, New Orleans Saints' coach J.D. Roberts sent in kicking specialist Tom Dempsey to try a field goal against the Detroit Lions. The 6-foot 1-inch, 265-pound Dempsey set up 10 yards behind the line of scrimmage, with holder Joe Scarpati kneeling at the 37. Jackie Burkett snapped the ball, Scarpati set it down, and Dempsey kicked.

The final gun sounded just before the cheers erupted from the 66,910 fans in Tulane's Sugar Bowl Stadium as the ball sailed through the uprights. The 63-yard kick was the longest field goal ever made in a National Football League game, surpassing the old record of 56 yards by Baltimore's Bert Rechichar against the Chicago Bears in 1953.

Dempsey, who was born without a right hand and with a clubbed right foot, the one he kicks with, said afterward he couldn't even see the goal posts he was kicking for. But he didn't have to see that far. "I saw the referee's hands go up and everybody started yelling and I knew it was good," Dempsey recounted happily.

Longest field goal: 63 yards, Tom Dempsey, New Orleans Saints, vs. Detroit Lions, November 8, 1970

In the course of his career, Green Bay's Bart Starr completed 57.42 percent of his passes.

Starr Billing

MIAMI, Florida, December 19, 1971—The last time Bart Starr walked off the field in the Orange Bowl, the grass was real and the glory was his. That was nearly four years ago, after the Packers had won their second straight Super Bowl.

Today, the 37-year-old Starr was a loser, for the Miami Dolphins had beaten Green Bay on artificial grass, 27–6, in the final game of the season, the last of Starr's career. The former Alabama quarterback—called a "coach on the field" in the Super Bowl years—underwent arm surgery before the 1971 season and had been used sparingly during the season. But coach Dan Devine went with him all the way today.

Starr was his usual proficient self, completing 13 of 22 passes for 126 yards. But he could do nothing to help the Packers put a touchdown on the scoreboard or avert a last-place finish in the NFC's "black and blue" Central Division with a record of four wins, eight losses, and two ties.

The accuracy of Starr today kept him first in that category among all the passers in NFL history, but he wasn't thinking of himself, statistics, or history after the game. "I'm sorry we couldn't put more points on the board. If we had, I'd feel better than I do now." Nonetheless, he and his passes stand tall in the record book.

Highest passing accuracy, career: 57.42 percent (1,808 of 3,149), Bart Starr, Green Bay Packers, 1956–71
Most consecutive passes with no interceptions: 294, Bart Starr, Green Bay Packers, 1964–65

Jack Be Nimble, Jack Be Quick

GREEN BAY, Wisconsin, September 24, 1972—The oldest record in the books was erased today by a quick and alert Jack Tatum and a misjudgment by the officials.

Tatum, playing safety for the Oakland Raiders, scooped up a bouncing football in one end zone and raced 104 yards down the sideline to the other end of the field for a touchdown that provided the margin of victory in Oakland's 20–14 victory over the Green Bay Packers. The officials ruled that the loose ball had been fumbled by MacArthur Lane and could legally be advanced. Lane, the Packers, some Oakland Raiders, and videotape replay later showed, however, that Lane had bobbled a pitchout and never had control of the ball. In that case, Tatum should not have been able to advance the ball.

But it was ruled a fumble, and so Tatum's name replaces that of George Halas of the Chicago Bears, who picked up a fumble and traveled 98 yards with it against Marion in an NFL game November 4, 1923.

Longest return of a recovered opponent's fumble: 104 yards, Jack Tatum, Oakland Raiders, vs. Green Bay Packers, September 24, 1972

Record-setting Don Maynard ended his career with the St. Louis Cardinals.

Catching It

PHILADELPHIA, Pennsylvania, September 16, 1973—Don Maynard, playing in an unfamiliar uniform in a city he has rarely visited, caught a Jim Hart pass today for 18 yards as the St. Louis Cardinals opened the season with a 34–23 victory over the Philadelphia Eagles.

The 6-foot 1-inch, 180-pound Maynard, who played his entire professional career in New York before coming to the Cardinals last week, was just a bench-warmer for St. Louis today. The 36-year-old receiver had been released by the New York Jets after spending 13 years with the franchise in the old American Football League and in the NFL after the merger. The cowboy from Texas Western also spent some time with the New York Giants in 1958.

Throughout his career, the sure-handed Maynard, who favored long sideburns and uniform No. 13, went on catching passes from quarterbacks ranging in talent from the forgettable Titans to the accuracy of Joe Namath and Jim Hart. His one catch today raised his career totals to 633 receptions for 11,834 yards, both professional records.

Most passes caught, career: 633, Don Maynard, New York Giants, 1958; New York Titans, 1960–62; New York Jets, 1963–72; St. Louis Cardinals, 1973

Most yards, pass receptions, career: 11,834, Don Maynard, New York Giants, 1958; New York Titans, 1960–62; New York Jets, 1963–72; St. Louis Cardinals, 1973

Dick Butkus of the Chicago Bears recovered his twenty-fifth fumble against the Houston Oilers.

Pouncing Bear

CHICAGO, Illinois, October 28, 1973—For the twenty-fifth time in his career, Chicago Bear middle linebacker Dick Butkus recovered an opponent's fumble, but for only the first time in his career did he recover a fumble for a touchdown.

The 6-foot 3-inch, 245-pound Butkus, who played center as well as linebacker at the University of Illinois 10 years ago, now holds the NFL record for most opponents' fumbles recovered. The mark came in a game today which saw the Bears hand the Houston Oilers their eighteenth straight defeat, 35–14, before a crowd of 43,755 in Wrigley Field.

Most opponents' fumbles recovered, career: 25, Dick Butkus, Chicago Bears, 1965–73

Adieu, Johnny U.

SAN DIEGO, California, November 4, 1973—Rookie Dan Fouts had been intercepted three times, the Chargers were being shut out and were losing, so San Diego coach Harland Svare went to his

Old No. 19, Johnny Unitas, ended his career in a San Diego uniform.

bench and called on a 40-year-old backup quarterback who hadn't played a minute of football in three weeks.

Johnny Unitas, who made No. 19 famous when he was leading the Baltimore Colts to so much of their glory, trotted onto the field wearing his distinctive high-top black football shoes, the same style he wore in Baltimore's sudden-death victory for the NFL championship in 1958, the same style he wore in the Colts' Super Bowl triumph more than a decade later.

But the Kansas City defense was the problem today, not the New York Giants or Dallas Cowboys. The Chiefs had prevented the Chargers from penetrating past the 38-yard line. Unitas went to work, and the Chargers picked up two quick first downs, mostly by running, but sparked by a 7-yard Unitas pass. Dropping back to pass again, Unitas was smothered by 285-pound Wilbur Young.

The old man was slow getting up and was in agonizing pain. Fouts came running onto the field and Unitas trotted off to the scattered, then swelling applause. It was the last time he would trot off a field in a player's uniform. He was in pain, but the bruised hip didn't bother him as much as the knowledge that he couldn't do anything to help San Diego avert a 19–0 loss.

Unitas' one pass, and one completion, raised his career totals and gave him these pro records:

Most passes attempted, career: 5,186, John Unitas, Baltimore Colts, 1956–72; San Diego Chargers, 1973
Most passes completed, career: 2,830, John Unitas, Baltimore Colts, 1956–72; San Diego Chargers, 1973
Most yards gained passing, career: 40,239, John Unitas, Baltimore Colts, 1956–72; San Diego Chargers, 1973
Most touchdown passes, career: 290, John Unitas, Baltimore Colts, 1956–72; San Diego Chargers, 1973

O.J. Is O.K.

NEW YORK, December 16, 1973—O.J. Simpson gained 200 yards on the ground against the New York Jets today and became the first ever to rush for more than 2,000 yards in a single National Football League season.

The Buffalo Bill running back smashed through the line for six yards late in the first quarter for his sixty-third yard of the game, which enabled him to break the old record of 1,863 set by Cleveland's Jim Brown in 1963. Simpson's record-breaking run came behind a block by rookie guard Joe DeLamielleure with 10:34 gone in the opening period at Shea Stadium. Simpson fumbled on the next play.

The 6-foot 1-inch, 212-pound Simpson, who had been a sprinter on the track team as well as a ball-carrier on the football team at the University of Southern California, carried the ball 34 times in Buffalo's 34–14 victory as he also established a season record of carrying the ball 323 times. His last carry, with 6:28 left in the game, was a 7-yard gain, which brought his total yardage for the day to 200 yards and for the season to 2,003. He left the game after that play and did not return.

Most yards gained rushing, season: 2,003, O.J. Simpson, Buffalo Bills, 1973

Most rushing attempts, season: 323, O.J. Simpson, Buffalo Bills, 1973

Buffalo's O.J. Simpson became the NFL's first 2,000-yard rusher against the New York Jets.

Return of the Cowboy

ST. LOUIS, Missouri, October 13, 1974—Dallas rookie Dennis Morgan opened the scoring today with a record-tying punt return, but it wasn't enough to bring victory to the Cowboys. The St. Louis Cardinals won their fifth straight game of the season, 31–28.

The 5-foot 11-inch, 200-pound Morgan, a 10th-round draft choice out of Western Illinois, gathered in a Hal Roberts punt on his own 2-yard line and weaved his way through the defense 98 yards for a touchdown.

The jaunt ties the NFL record for longest return of a punt, shared by Gil LeFevre of the old Cincinnati Reds and Charlie West of the Minnesota Vikings.

Longest punt return: 98 yards, Dennis Morgan, Dallas Cowboys, vs. St. Louis Cardinals, October 13, 1974 (Ties Charlie West, Minnesota Vikings, vs. Washington Redskins, November 3, 1968 and Gil LeFevre, Cincinnati Reds, vs. Brooklyn Dodgers, December 3, 1933)

What's the Rush?

NEW YORK, October 20, 1974—For the second time in less than a year, a running back has run for a record against the New York Jets here in Shea Stadium. Last December, Buffalo's O.J. Simpson gained 200 yards and became the first man to gain more than 2,000 yards in a single NFL season.

Today it was Baltimore's Lydell Mitchell who ran into the record book. The 5-foot 11-inch, 200-pounder who had teamed with Franco Harris on Penn State's bowl teams in 1969, 1970, and 1971, carried the ball 40 times in helping the Colts to a 35–20 upset of the Jets.

Mitchell, who still holds a couple of single-season scoring records in the collegiate ranks, gained 156 yards on his 40 carries. His longest run was for only 12 yards, but his efforts were crucial. He carried the ball on third down on eight different occasions, and seven times he picked up the first-down yardage.

Most rushing attempts, game: 40, Lydell Mitchell, Baltimore Colts, vs. New York Jets, October 20, 1974

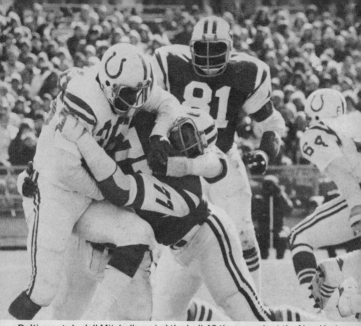

Baltimore's Lydell Mitchell carried the ball 40 times against the New York Jets.

Handy Andy

CINCINNATI, Ohio, November 10, 1974—Cincinnati quarterback Ken Anderson threw himself into the game 100 percent today and came out of it with a large headache, an NFL record, and an upset victory for the Bengals over the first-place Pittsburgh Steelers.

The 25-year-old Anderson, who played collegiate ball at Augustana in Rock Island, Illinois, connected on his first eight passes of the day. These completions ran his string to 16 in a row, as he was on his way to completing a record percentage of passes in a game.

Anderson was on target most of the day, but in the third quarter he was knocked almost unconscious on a vicious out-of-bounds head tackle. He was flat on his back for nearly five minutes, but later returned to the game where he continued his passing wizardry, finishing the day by completing 22 of 24 passes for a 91 percent

Cincinnati's Ken Anderson completed 91 percent of his passes in a game against Pittsburgh.

efficiency rating, topping the 86.2 percent achieved by Oakland's Ken Stabler on 25 of 29 last season.

Anderson also helped preserve the 17–10 victory for Cincinnati when, with only 4:04 remaining, he made a head-first but game-saving tackle on Pittsburgh's Mike Wagner who was headed for the end zone after picking up a Bengal fumble and running 69 yards with it.

Highest pass completion percentage, game (minimum 20 attempts): 91 percent (22 of 24), Ken Anderson, Cincinnati Bengals, vs. Pittsburgh Steelers, November 10, 1974

BASEBALL

Iron Hoss

NEW YORK, October 27, 1884—Pitching for the third day in a row, as he has done so often during the season, Charley "Hoss" Radbourne hurled his third successive victory in leading the National League champion Providence Grays to a clean sweep in their playoff with the New York Metropolitans, American Association champions.

The sweep climaxed a phenomenal season for Radbourne, in which he won 60 games and lost 12 while Providence was racking up an 84–28 record. Using an overhand delivery which begins with a running start, Radbourne led the league with 441 strikeouts, a 1.38 earned-run average, 73 complete games in 75 starts, and 678⅔ innings pitched. In 15 of the games in which he didn't pitch, he was in the outfield, from where he could be called to the mound if necessary. Substitutions are not allowed, even for pitchers, once the game is under way.

The 29-year-old Radbourne was not even the team's starting pitcher at the beginning of the season, but took over after Charley Sweeney was dismissed for insubordination. Radbourne's success—which included 18 straight victories during one stretch—was not without agonizing effort. When he woke up in the mornings, Hoss couldn't even raise his right arm high enough to comb his hair. In order to warm up for a game, he would arrive at the field two hours before the rest of the team and start throwing, his pitches going only a few feet at first. When his teammates arrived, Radbourne would be standing on second base ready to peg the ball home.

Most victories, season: 60, Charles Radbourne, Providence (NL), 1884

Duffy's Day

PITTSBURGH, Pennsylvania, September 29, 1894—The hitters have won the battle of the pitching rubber. Pint-sized Hugh Duffy laced two hits today as Boston defeated Pittsburgh, 6–5, and the Beantown centerfielder finished the season with a .438 batting average. The only league-leader to have a higher average was Tip O'Neill, who was credited with a .492 in 1887, the year bases on balls were counted as hits.

Duffy, who stands 5-feet 7-inches and weighs 165 pounds, has always been a good hitter, batting well over .300 each year since he came into the league in 1890. This season he led the National League in hits with 237; doubles with 51; home runs, 18; runs batted in, 143; and slugging, .690. In addition, back on June 18, he tied a major league mark by reaching first base three times in one inning.

Much of the credit for Duffy's success—and that of the other hitters, too—must go to the rule implemented this year that moved the pitchers back to a distance of 60-feet 6-inches from home plate and required the hurlers to work from a 12-inch by 4-inch rubber slab.

Highest batting average, season: .438, Hugh Duffy, Boston (NL), 1894

The Kid Shoots for Seven

BALTIMORE, Maryland, September 27, 1897—People came from miles around to see the showdown. There were 3,000 men on the rooftops, plus 500 or so who hopped on and off the fences, depending upon the proximity of constables. And inside the ballpark, 25,390 had paid for the privilege of seeing the Bostons and Baltimores battle. Another 1,000 were inside the gates *gratis*, gaining access when a bleacher gate gave way under the crush of the crowd.

The showdown came, as expected, and The Kid won. Charles A. "Kid" Nichols, as nifty a righthander as baseball has seen, picked up his thirtieth victory of the season, giving him a record seven consecutive 30-game seasons. But what was more important to The Kid was that it was the second time in this three-game series that he had pitched a victory against the Orioles. This gave Boston a game and a half lead over the defending champions in the National League pennant race.

It wasn't one of Nichols' better efforts, although he did win his thirtieth game and extend his record. He gave up 13 hits, three walks, and hit an Oriole as Boston won, 19–10. The Kid had a little offensive punch of his own, getting three hits, including one in the seventh inning when Boston rallied for nine runs and put the game out of reach.

Most seasons 30 or more victories: 7, Charles A. Nichols, Boston (NL), 1891–97

"Big Ed" Walsh of the Chicago White Sox pitched 464 innings in 1908.

Rubber Arm

CHICAGO, Illinois, October 6, 1908—The White Sox called on Ed Walsh for the fourth game in a row, but the big righthander didn't have anything left as Detroit went on to win the game, 7–0, and clinch the American League pennant.

Walsh, who had a 39–15 record in 66 games this season, came on in relief after Detroit jumped on Guy White in the first inning. Before Walsh could retire the side, Detroit had a 4–0 lead. The 3⅔ innings Walsh pitched today raised his season's total to 464, a modern record.

Walsh had pitched Chicago into contention, winning a complete game victory, 6–1, over Detroit yesterday to pull his team to within one-half game of the Tigers. In the game before that, Walsh recorded his seventh save of the season as he came in with the bases loaded late in the game to preserve a 3–2 victory over Cleveland. Four days ago, also against Cleveland, Walsh pitched a four-hitter, struck out 15, and walked only one, but lost, 1–0, as

Addie Joss hurled a perfect no-hit, no-run game against the White Sox.

In addition to innings pitched, games, victories, and saves, Walsh led the AL with 269 strikeouts, 42 complete games, and 11 shutouts.

Most innings pitched, season (since 1900): 464, Edward A. Walsh, Chicago (AL), 1908

Cy Young won 511 games.

Cy Young's Last Game

BROOKLYN, New York, October 6, 1911—The Brooklyn Superbas drove Cy Young off the mound and into retirement with an eight-run barrage in the seventh inning of today's game with the Boston Rustlers.

Denton True "Cy" Young, holder of the major league records for both most-games-won and most-games-lost, was touched for eight straight hits and eight runs in the second game of a double-header at Washington Park. After Brooklyn's Bob Coulson doubled, Young threw his glove down in disgust and walked off the mound. The Superbas had broken up a 3–3 tie when pinch-hitter Zack Wheat singled home Otto Miller, who had tripled. The floodgates were open and Brooklyn went on to rout the team with the worst record in the National League, 13–3.

Young, 44 years old and fat, finished the year with four wins and five losses in the National League, to go with the 3–4 record he compiled with Cleveland in the AL earlier this season. It was the 315th defeat in his 22-year career, and goes with his 511 victories, both totals unapproached by anyone else. Young is the only man to win 200 or more games in each league, playing with Cleveland and Boston in the American League between 1901 and the middle of this season. He won 222 games during that period. Young broke into the major leagues with Cleveland in 1890, when that city had a National League franchise. He also played with St. Louis in addition to his brief stint with the Rustlers this season.

Before the season even began, Young indicated his desire to quit playing. He was trying to lose weight at Hot Springs, Arkansas, while avoiding spring training, a ritual he had long detested. It was there that he made his annual retirement announcement. This time he meant it.

Most games started, career: 818, Denton "Cy" Young, Cleveland (NL), 1890–98; St. Louis (NL), 1899–1900; Boston (AL), 1901–08; Cleveland (AL), 1909–11; Boston (NL), 1911

Most complete games, career: 751, Denton "Cy" Young, Cleveland (NL), 1890–98; St. Louis (NL), 1899–1900; Boston (AL), 1901–08; Cleveland (AL), 1909–11; Boston (NL), 1911

Most games won, career: 511, Denton "Cy" Young, Cleveland (NL), 1890–98; St. Louis (NL), 1899–1900; Boston (AL), 1901–08; Cleveland (AL), 1909–11; Boston (NL), 1911

Most games lost, career: 315, Denton "Cy" Young, Cleveland (NL), 1890–98; St. Louis (NL), 1899–1900; Boston (AL), 1901–08; Cleveland (AL), 1909–11; Boston (NL), 1911

Instant Major Leaguers

PHILADELPHIA, Pennsylvania, May 18, 1912—The crowd of 20,000 thought the game was a joke, the Philadelphia players loved the batting practice, and pitcher Aloysius Travers worked his way into the record book.

With the regular Detroit players on strike, the team's management faced a stiff fine from the league if nine players were not in uniform for today's game. The major league team that was on the field in Detroit uniforms turned out to be several members of St. Joseph's College team, other assorted amateurs, and a couple of former big-leaguers on the Detroit executive payroll.

The regular Detroit players had warmed up before the game, then refused to take the field. They were protesting the suspension of Ty Cobb by American League president Ban Johnson after Cobb had climbed into the stands to go at it with a fan who had been riding him particularly hard in New York three days ago.

It took only an hour and 55 minutes for Philadelphia to bang out 25 hits off Travers, score 24 runs, and steal eight bases. Travers, a former star on the St. Joseph's team, went the full eight innings and received little fielding support from his mates, who committed nine errors. Offensively, Detroit managed four hits and two runs. Each recruit picked up $50 for his efforts.

Most runs allowed by a pitcher, game: 24, Aloysius Travers, Detroit (AL), May 18, 1912

Rube the Great

CHICAGO, Illinois, July 8, 1912—He knew it wouldn't last. New York Giant pitcher Rube Marquard had opened the season with a victory over Brooklyn. He won his next game, too. And the one after that. It kept going that way through April, May, and June. Five days ago, on July 3, at the Polo Grounds in New York, Marquard gave up nine hits, five walks, and had to deal with men on base in every inning but one. His teammates worked only four hits off Napoleon Rucker, but the Giants managed to squeak by Brooklyn with a 2–1 victory, giving Rube his nineteenth consecutive triumph.

He hadn't lost a game and the season was nearly half over. The victory tied him with Tim Keefe of the old New York team who, back in 1888, had the advantage of pitching much closer to the plate.

Chicago pitcher Jimmy Lavender came into today's duel with Marquard riding a modest streak of his own: 34 consecutive innings of shutout pitching. The Giants ended that string in the third inning, but Lavender had the last laugh as the Cubs scored six runs off Marquard in six innings before the Giant lefty was lifted for a pinch-hitter. Heinie Zimmerman and Joe Tinker led the Chicago attack and then played errorless ball in support of Lavender. The Cub hurler yielded only five hits as Chicago ended Marquard's skein with a 6–2 victory.

Most consecutive games won, start of season: 19, Richard W. "Rube" Marquard, New York (NL), April 11 to July 3, 1912

Rube Marquard of the New York Giants won 19 straight games from the start of the 1912 season.

Pittsburgh's J. Owen "Chief" Wilson hit 36 triples in 1912.

Triple Threat

CINCINNATI, Ohio, October 6, 1912—Pittsburgh centerfielder
John Owen "Chief" Wilson rapped out a single and a triple to lead

a 19-hit attack in a 16–6 victory over Cincinnati. For Wilson, who finished the season with a .304 batting average, the triple was his thirty-sixth of the season, an all-time major league record for three-base hits.

The native of Austin, Texas, has been hitting the ball well all season and used his speed to stretch many a double into a triple. Earlier this year he set a major league record by hitting six triples in five consecutive games between June 17 and June 20.

Most triples, season: 36, J. Owen Wilson, Pittsburgh (NL), 1912
Most triples, five consecutive games: 6, J. Owen Wilson, Pittsburgh
(NL), June 17–20, 1912

Goose Eggs in the Clutch

PHILADELPHIA, Pennsylvania, October 8, 1913—Christy Mathewson singled home the first run of the game today as the New York Giants went on to beat Philadelphia, 3–0, and tie the World Series at one game each. The shutout was Mathewson's first in this series, and with the three he pitched in the 1905 Series against these same Athletics, gives him the all-time record of four shutouts in World Series competition.

In winning today, Mathewson gave up eight hits, walked one, struck out five, and was hurt by two errors, one of which almost cost him the shutout.

Amos Strunk led off the ninth with a single and Jack Barry followed with a sacrifice bunt. Larry Doyle made a throwing error on the bunt, and the A's had men on second and third with none out. Hooks Wiltse, substituting for the injured Fred Merkle at first, made a sensational stop of a smash by Johnny Lapp and threw out Strunk at the plate. With Barry on third, pitcher Eddie Plank sizzled another one at Wiltse, who again threw home, and Barry was tagged out in a rundown. Danny Murphy then grounded out, pitcher to first, to end the game.

The 33-year-old Mathewson thus went into the record books again, adding another line to go with his modern NL mark of 37 victories in 1908 and his record of 11 seasons pitching 300 or more innings.

World Series:
Most shutouts, career: 4, Christy Mathewson, New York (NL), 1905
(3) and 1913 (1)

The New York Giants' Christy Mathewson pitched four World Series shut-outs.

Boston's Rabbit Maranville helped end the 1916 New York Giants' 26-game winning streak.

Streaking Giants

NEW YORK, September 30, 1916—There was good news and bad news for the 38,000 fans who showed up at the Polo Grounds today. The good news was that Rube Benton pitched a one-hitter as the Giants beat Boston, 4–0, to extend their winning streak to 26 games. The bad news was that Boston won the second game of the doubleheader, 8–2, to snap the streak.

The loss came as Rabbit Maranville turned in one fielding gem after another at shortstop in support of George Tyler's pitching in the night cap. The death knell for the streak was sounded in the seventh inning when the Braves scored five runs. The key blows were back-to-back home runs by Carlisle "Red" Smith and Sherry Magee off the Giants' Slim Sallee.

During the 26-game streak, which began September 7, the Giants beat every other team in the league at least once, although all the games were at home. But despite the string, today's loss eliminated the McGrawmen from any chance of winning the pennant.

Most consecutive victories: 26, New York (NL), September 7–30, 1916

Three-Bag Man

DETROIT, Michigan, September 22, 1916—Sam Crawford, the greatest triples-hitter baseball has ever known, stroked the 312th three-bagger of his career today to spark Detroit to a 6–5 victory over Washington.

Though overshadowed by teammate Ty Cobb when it comes to public acclaim, Crawford has had some distinctions, such as being the only man ever to lead each major league in home runs. In addition, the lefthanded-hitting outfielder shares the American League's single season record for triples with 26, when he hit that many in 1914.

Despite his proclivity for hitting triples, Crawford has never hit two in one inning nor four in one game, achievements which would have earned him another line in the record book.

A native of Wahoo, Nebraska, Crawford broke into the majors with Cincinnati in 1899, where he led the National League in home runs in 1901 with 16. He came to Detroit in 1903 and led the AL sluggers with seven home runs in 1908.

Most triples, career: 312, Sam Crawford, Cincinnati (NL), 1899–1902; Detroit (AL), 1903–1917

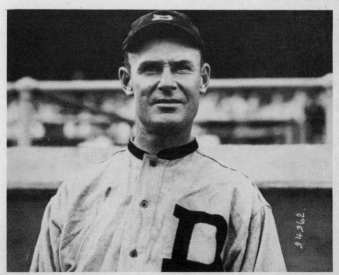

Detroit's Sam ''Wahoo'' Crawford hit 312 triples in his career.

Philadelphia's Grover Cleveland Alexander shut out 16 opponents in 1916.

Mr. 000 000 000

PHILADELPHIA, Pennsylvania, October 2, 1916—"Alexander the Great" is what they are calling Grover Cleveland "Pete" Alexander today after the 29-year-old righthander hurled a record sixteenth shutout for his thirty-third victory of the season. Pitching in the hitters' paradise called Baker Bowl, Alexander has had only 11 losses for the Phillies this season.

In today's 2–0 triumph, Pete scattered three singles among Boston hitters and allowed no runner to get past second base, as he gave up no walks and struck out four. A 4–1 loss in the second game of the doubleheader dimmed the record-book performance by Alexander, since it kept Philadelphia one game behind league-leading Brooklyn.

For the purists, Alexander's feat is only a modern record, since back in 1876 George Bradley is credited with 16 shutouts for St. Louis. But he was pitching from the old 50-foot distance rather than the modern 60-foot 6-inch range.

Most shutouts, season: 16, Grover C. Alexander, Philadelphia (NL), 1916

Babe Ruth of the Boston Red Sox pitched more innings in a World Series game than anyone else.

Babe on the Mound

BOSTON, Massachusetts, October 9, 1916—Boston pitcher George "Babe" Ruth gave up a first-inning home run to Hi Myers and then held Brooklyn to only five hits after that for 14 innings as

53

Boston took a 2–0 lead in the World Series with a 2–1 triumph here today. In going the distance, Ruth established a record for most innings pitched in a World Series game.

Ruth, hit hard in the first five innings before settling down, struck out three and walked three as Brooklyn left five men on base. This was the first Series victory for the lefthanded Ruth, who compiled a 23–12 record during the regular season while leading the American League with nine shutouts and a 1.75 earned-run average, a record low for a lefthanded pitcher.

World Series:
Most innings pitched, game: 14, George H. "Babe" Ruth, Boston (AL), October 9, 1916

On and On and On and On and

BOSTON, Massachusetts, May 1, 1920—Communist-inspired May Day riots were the rule of the day in most major cities (three

Brooklyn's Leon Cadore (left) and Boston's Joe Oeschger went the distance in baseball's longest game.

persons were killed in riots in Paris), but here in Boston the activity was much more restrained. For a record 26 innings, the Brooklyn Robins and Boston Braves sparred in an effort to win a baseball game before a chilled crowd of about 2,000. When it became too dark to play, the score was still tied, 1–1, as it had been at the end of every inning since the sixth.

Pitchers Joe Oeschger for Boston and Leon Cadore for Brooklyn went the entire distance, with Oeschger having somewhat the better of it by allowing only nine hits, including one that led to a Brooklyn run in the fifth inning. The Braves rapped 15 hits off Cadore, but could pick up only one run, in the home half of the sixth.

Only twice did it look as though the game might have a decisive outcome. In the ninth, Boston filled the bases with one out when Charlie Pick grounded to Ivy Olson, who tagged Ray Powell on the basepath and threw to first in time to double the batter. End of threat.

Boston had a scare in the seventeenth inning when Oeschger allowed two hits in one inning for the only time in the game. The bases were full of Robins when Rowdy Elliot knocked the ball back to the mound. Oeschger threw home to force Zack Wheat, but the relay to first was fumbled by Walt Holke. The first baseman retrieved the ball and whipped it home in time for catcher Hank Gowdy to tag Ed Konetchy, trying to score from second on the play.

Most innings pitched, game: 26, Leon J. Cadore, Brooklyn (NL), May 1, 1920, and Joseph C. Oeschger, Boston (NL), May 1, 1920
Most batsmen faced, game: 97, Leon J. Cadore, Brooklyn (NL), May 1, 1920
Longest game in innings: 26, Brooklyn vs. Boston (NL), May 1, 1920

George Sisler of the St. Louis Browns rapped 257 hits in one season.

Sizzling Sisler

ST. LOUIS, Missouri, October 3, 1920—George Sisler won the
battle of St. Louis today, battering the scandal-scarred Chicago
White Sox for three hits in a 16–7 victory for the Browns.

Sisler, the former University of Michigan athlete, showed he
was as adroit with the bat as he is with a glove, finishing the season
with a record 257 hits and a .407 batting average. He was also
among the leading fielders in the league, topping them all in assists by a first baseman.

Sisler far outdistanced the National League's leading batter,
Rogers Hornsby of the crosstown Cardinals, who wound up hitting .370 for the season. Playing in 154 games, Sisler scored 137
runs this season in 631 times at bat.

Revelations of the 1919 World Series scandal came out this
year, and were followed by charges that some White Sox players
had dumped this season's pennant. But the way they played today
it didn't look as though the White Sox were good enough to throw
anything, as the Browns pounded out 18 hits in the assault.

Most hits, one season: 257, George H. Sisler, St. Louis (AL), 1920

Boom-Boom Bottomley

BROOKLYN, New York, September 16, 1924—Brooklyn's pennant express was ambushed today as Jim Bottomley rapped six
hits—including home runs in two consecutive times at bat—and
drove in a major league record 12 runs. Bottomley also scored another run, thus having a direct hand in 13 of the 17 St. Louis runs
in the Cardinals' 17–3 victory.

Bottomley treated five Brooklyn pitchers with equal disdain,
getting at least one hit off each. Sunny Jim started his barrage with
a bases-loaded single off Rube Ehrhardt in the first inning, driving
in two runs. He doubled home a run in the next inning before belt-
ing a grand-slam home run in the fourth, to make the score 9–1.
Next time up, in the sixth, he socked a two-run blast, followed by a
two-run single in the seventh. Bottomley ended the day's work by
singling home Rogers Hornsby in the ninth inning for the final St.
Louis tally.

The Brooklyn rooters were of course dismayed, but none as
much as Wilbert Robertson, who was in the crowd of 20,000. Rob-

ertson had set the old record of 11 runs batted in with the old Baltimore Orioles in 1892 against, you guessed it, St. Louis.

Most runs batted in, game: 12, James L. Bottomley, St. Louis (NL), September 16, 1924

End of the Line

WASHINGTON, D.C., September 21, 1927—The Big Train made his last stop today, running out of smoke in the fourth inning

Washington's Walter Johnson struck out 3,508 and pitched 113 shutouts.

against the St. Louis Browns. If Walter Johnson's fastball wasn't what it once was, his competitive spirit remained intact.

Recovering from a broken leg sustained in spring training, Johnson worked hard to achieve a 5-5 record in his final season. Today's game didn't figure in it, since Washington came back to win, 10-7, after Walter left the mound with one out in the fourth inning. He also missed a chance to add to his record total of 113 career shutouts. But Johnson did strike out two Browns, to raise his major league record total to 3,508.

Johnson came into the major leagues after earning a reputation in the semipro Snake River Valley League, striking out 166 batters in 11 games as a teen-ager. He went directly to Washington, and, disdaining the overhand pitching style favored by most speedballers, showed he could throw smoke from a motion somewhere between sidearm and three-quarter arm delivery.

Despite his brilliance, Johnson was surrounded by mediocrity and he didn't play in a World Series until 1924, well past his prime, at the age of 36. His effectiveness was not just in his blazing fast ball, but in his control, too. In 1913, perhaps his best year, the Big Train won 36, lost only 7, and walked only 38 men all season in compiling an earned-run average of 1.14, a record for a right-handed pitcher.

Most strikeouts, career: 3,508, Walter Johnson, Washington (AL), 1907–27

Most shutouts, career: 113, Walter Johnson, Washington (AL), 1907–27

Most American League games started: 666, Walter Johnson, Washington, 1907–27

Most shutouts lost, career: 65, Walter Johnson, Washington (AL), 1907–27

Most consecutive seasons pitching for one team: 21, Walter Johnson, Washington (AL), 1907–27

Most American League games won: 416, Walter Johnson, Washington, 1907–27

Most American League games lost: 279, Walter Johnson, Washington, 1907–27

Most innings pitched, one league: 5,924, Walter Johnson, Washington (AL), 1907–27

Most hit batsmen, career: 205, Walter Johnson, Washington (AL), 1907–27

Most batters faced, one league, career: 23,200, Walter Johnson, Washington (AL), 1907–27

Ty Cobb ended his career with a .367 batting average.

Cobb's Corner of the Record Book

NEW YORK, September 11, 1928—A crowd of 50,000 was on hand in Yankee Stadium to see an historic moment in baseball. They watched the defending World Champion New York Yankees defeat Philadelphia, 5-3, and extend their lead to 2½ games over the Athletics. The margin of victory was provided in the bottom of the eighth inning when, with Lou Gehrig on second, Babe Ruth smashed a home run off Lefty Grove.

But the historic moment came in the top of the ninth inning when Ty Cobb was sent up to pinch-hit for third baseman Jimmy Dykes. The 42-year-old Georgia Peach popped a fly ball past third that was gathered in by shortstop Mark Koenig. It was Ty Cobb's last time at bat in the major leagues.

The inauspicious swan song didn't damage Cobb's average very much, for he had 114 hits in 353 times at bat this season for a healthy .323 average. And it in no way diminished his career totals, which included a record .367 lifetime batting average, only one of his several major league marks.

Highest batting average, career: .367, Tyrus R. Cobb, Detroit (AL), 1905-26, Philadelphia (AL), 1927-28

60

Most seasons leading major leagues in batting: 11, Tyrus R. Cobb, Detroit (AL), 1907, 1909–15, 1917–19

Most consecutive seasons leading major leagues in batting: 7, Tyrus R. Cobb, Detroit (AL), 1909–15

Most seasons batting .300 or better: 23, Tyrus R. Cobb, Detroit (AL), 1905–26, Philadelphia (AL), 1927–28

Most plate appearances, career: 12,713, Tyrus R. Cobb, Detroit (AL), 1905–26, Philadelphia (AL), 1927–28

Most seasons leading major league in hits: 7, Tyrus R. Cobb, Detroit (AL), 1907, 1909, 1911–12, 1915–17, 1919

Most hits, career: 4,191, Tyrus R. Cobb, Detroit (AL), 1905–26, Philadelphia (AL), 1927–28

Most games, five or more hits: 50, Tyrus R. Cobb, Detroit (AL), 1905–26, Philadelphia (AL), 1927–28

Most singles, career (since 1900): 892, Tyrus R. Cobb, Detroit (AL), 1905–26, Philadelphia (AL), 1927–28

Most times stolen home: 34, Tyrus R. Cobb, Detroit (AL), 1905–26, Philadelphia (AL), 1927–28

Ruthian Feat

ST. LOUIS, Missouri, October 9, 1928—Playing hurt and to the accompaniment of boos, hisses, jeers, and a few bottles from the leftfield stands, Babe Ruth continued his torrid hitting and swatted three home runs today to lead the New York Yankees to a 7–3 World Series victory over St. Louis.

The home runs accounted for Ruth's only runs batted in during the Series as the Yankees swept all four games. Ruth's 10 hits in 16 times at bat gave him a record .625 batting average. The Cardinal pitchers—Billy Sherdel, Grover "Pete" Alexander, Jesse Haines, Syl Johnson—could do nothing with the Babe as the Yankees won the first two games in New York, 4–1 and 9–3, before taking the pair here, by identical 7–3 scores.

Ruth's three home runs, the second time he has accomplished this feat in a World Series game, helped the Yanks to a team record nine for the Series. Lou Gehrig, who also clouted a circuit blast today, had four round-trippers in the Series, tying the Babe's 1926 mark. Thanks to the Bambino being on base so often, Gehrig, who followed him in the batting order, drove in nine runs, a record for a four-game series.

Ruth played the entire Series with a bum knee, but the injury didn't prevent him from bringing the caterwauling fans in the stands to near silence when he made a spectacular one-handed, knee-sliding grab of a fly ball to end the game and the Series.

World Series:
Highest batting average: .625, George H. "Babe" Ruth, New York (AL), 1928
Highest slugging average: 1.727, Lou Gehrig, New York (AL), 1928
Most total bases, one game: 12, George H "Babe" Ruth, New York (AL), October 9, 1928 (Ties his own record of October 6, 1926)
Most home runs, one game: 3, George H. "Babe" Ruth, New York (AL), October 9, 1928 (Ties his own record of October 6, 1926)

Hack Performance

CHICAGO, Illinois, September 28, 1930—In an era when American Leaguers are dominating the hitting statistics, Chicago Cub centerfielder Lewis "Hack" Wilson drove in two runs with a pair of singles in today's season finale to push his RBI total to a record 190 for the season as the Cubs outslugged Cincinnati, 13–11. In yesterday's game, Wilson smacked his fifty-fifth and fifty-sixth home runs of the season to establish a National League record.

Nicknamed for the popular strongman and wrestler, Hackenschmidt, Wilson is a stocky, broadfaced, no-neck righthanded batter who can hit with power. This season is the fourth time in five years that he has led the NL in home runs, and the second straight season he has driven in more than 180 runs, the only player in senior circuit history to accomplish this.

Most runs batted in, season: 190, Lewis R. "Hack" Wilson, Chicago (NL), 1930

The Chicago Cubs' Hack Wilson holds the major league record with 190 runs batted in.

Lou Gehrig congratulates Babe Ruth in the Yankees' record-smashing 1932 World Series.

Fence Busters

CHICAGO, Illinois, October 2, 1932—Murderers Row did it again, establishing offensive records left and right as the New York Yankees won their twelfth consecutive World Series game today, downing the Chicago Cubs, 13–6.

As in 1927 and 1928, the Yanks were led by Babe Ruth and Lou Gehrig in sweeping their National League foes in four games.

New York's team batting average of .313 is a record for a four-game series, as was Chicago's .253 for a losing team.

In addition to the team records, there were some distinctive individual performances. In yesterday's third game, for example, as Babe Ruth strode up to the plate in the fifth inning, a lemon rolled across his path. Glaring at pitcher Charlie Root, Ruth took two balls and two strikes, pointing after each pitch to a spot over the right field fence where he intended to hit the ball. The Babe was off in his prediction, however, as the ball sailed over the fence in dead center. Also in yesterday's game, Yankee pitcher George Pipgras struck out a record five times in five plate appearances, while the Yanks were winning, 7–5.

In today's finale, Lou Gehrig scored twice, each time on a Tony Lazzeri home run, to tie Babe Ruth's record for nine runs scored in a series, a record for a series of any number of games.

Some of the other marks established for a four-game series were one- and two-team records for times at bat, runs, hits, total bases, singles, home runs, runs batted in, walks and hit batsmen. The big hitters for the Cubs were Riggs Stephenson, Frank Demaree, Kiki Cuyler, Charlie Grimm and Billy Herman.

World Series:
Most runs, individual: 9, Lou Gehrig, New York (AL), 1932 (Ties George H. "Babe" Ruth, New York (AL), 1928)
Highest slugging average, both teams: .459, New York (AL) and Chicago (NL), 1932
Most series batting .300 or higher: 6, George H. "Babe" Ruth, New York (AL), 1921, 1923, 1926, 1928, 1932
Highest slugging average, career: .744, George H. "Babe" Ruth, Boston (AL), 1915–16, 1918; New York (AL), 1921–23, 1926–28, 1932
Most strikeouts, batter, one game: 5, George Pipgras, New York (AL), October 1, 1932

King Carl

NEW YORK, July 10, 1934—The second annual All-Star Game, played before a crowd of 48,363, was a hitters' contest, with the American League finally winning, 9–7. But you couldn't prove it by Carl Hubbell.

The New York Giant lefthander, playing before the home fans in his home ball park, looked like he was in for a short day's work

The New York Giants' Carl Hubbell struck out five consecutive batters in the 1934 All-Star Game.

at the Polo Grounds when AL leadoff batter Charlie Gehringer singled and Heinie Manush walked. Up came Babe Ruth, whose home run accounted for the AL's 4–2 triumph in last year's inaugural All-Star Game in Chicago. With Yankee fans trying to outshout Giant rooters on Coogan's Bluff, Ruth took a called third strike from Hubbell.

Lou Gehrig was the next batter, bringing a regular season batting average of .370 into the game. Gehrig went down swinging as Gehringer and Manush executed a double steal. Next, it was clutch-hitting Jimmy Foxx's turn. Foxx was the AL leader in homers, runs batted in, and slugging percentage for the past two seasons. Hubbell struck Foxx out on five pitches.

After Frankie Frisch homered to give the Nationals a 1–0 lead, Hubbell faced Al Simmons to start the second inning. Another .350 hitter, Simmons whiffed on four pitches. The stadium was abuzz as shortstop Joe Cronin walked toward the plate. The playing manager of the Washington Senators was also manager of the AL All-Star squad. A pesky hitter, Cronin had driven in 72 runs during the season. He, too, fell before Hubbell's pitching mastery as he became the fifth straight strikeout victim, an All-Star Game record. Bill Dickey broke Hubbell's string with a single, but King Carl came right back and struck out opposing pitcher Vernon "Lefty" Gomez.

All-Star Game:
Most consecutive strikeouts: 5, Carl Hubbell, New York (NL), July 10, 1934

The Babe Bows Out

BOSTON, Massachusetts, June 2, 1935—As dramatic off the field as he is flamboyant on the baseball diamond, Babe Ruth precipitated a controversy that ended in his unconditional release today from the Boston Braves. Team president Judge Emil E. Fuchs made the decision after Ruth had attended a shipboard party in violation of curfew regulations set by manager Bill McKechnie.

The 41-year-old Ruth had been nothing more than a drawing card for the hapless Braves, wallowing in the National League cellar. Other teams in the league were holding "Babe Ruth Days" in an effort to boost attendance. A chronic knee injury had reduced the Bambino's playing time and in his last game, May 30, in Philadelphia, he played left field only briefly and failed to get a hit in his one time at bat. The day before he settled for a pair of walks. But only a week ago, Ruth showed he was still capable of destroying pitchers.

Playing at Forbes Field in Pittsburgh, the Babe smashed three home runs off Pirate hurlers Red Lucas and Guy Bush. They were the 712th, 713th, and 714th home runs of his career, which began as a lefthanded pitcher with the Boston Red Sox in 1914.

The Sultan of Swat, Il Bambino, the Babe, or George Herman Ruth, they all started out in Baltimore, where as a 7-year-old street urchin he was sent to St. Mary's Industrial Home. He never lost the rough edges of his origins, although he won the hearts and respect of America. An early Boston teammate, Harry Hooper, recalled, "Sometimes I still can't believe what I saw, this 19-year-old kid crude, poorly educated . . . gradually transformed into the idol of American youth and the symbol of baseball the world over."

This was the Babe in his heyday, hitting his sixtieth home run with the Yankees in 1927.

Highest slugging average, lifetime: .692, George H. "Babe" Ruth, Boston (AL), 1914–19; New York (AL), 1920–34; Boston (NL), 1935

Most bases on balls, lifetime: 2,056, George H. "Babe" Ruth, Boston (AL), 1914–19; New York (AL), 1920–34; Boston (NL), 1935

Most seasons, 50 or more home runs: 4, George H. "Babe" Ruth, New York (AL), 1920–21, 1927–28

Most seasons 40 or more home runs: 11, George H. "Babe" Ruth, New York (AL), 1920–21, 1923–24, 1926–34

Most seasons leading major leagues in home runs: 11, George H. "Babe" Ruth, Boston (AL), 1918–19, New York (AL), 1920–21, 1923–24, 1926–29, 1931

Most seasons leading major leagues in runs scored: 8, George H. "Babe" Ruth, Boston (AL), 1919; New York (AL), 1920–21, 1923–24, 1926–28

Most seasons leading major leagues in runs batted in: 5, George H. "Babe" Ruth, New York (AL), 1920–21, 1923, 1926, 1928

Lefty Is Right

WASHINGTON, D.C., July 7, 1937—Vernon "Lefty" Gomez, pitching for the fourth time in the five All-Star Games that have been played, did the hurling and Yankee teammate Lou Gehrig did the hitting as the American League beat the Nationals, 8–3, before a crowd of 31,391 that included President Franklin Roosevelt in Griffith Stadium. The victory was credited to Gomez, a record third time he has been the winning pitcher in the All-Star Game.

Starters in the 1937 All-Star Game: Vernon "Lefty" Gomez (left) and Dizzy Dean.

With Gehrig driving in four runs on a homer and a double, Gomez kept the NL at bay by allowing only one hit and walking none in his three-inning stint as starting pitcher. In 1935, Lefty worked a record six innings in the All-Star Game and allowed only three hits as the AL won, 4–1, in Cleveland. Gomez was also the winning pitcher in the first All-Star Game in 1933, which the AL won, 4–2, in Chicago.

National League starter Dizzy Dean accepted the blame for today's loss. "I shook [Gabby] Hartnett off twice and I was belted each time," Dean lamented after the game. One of those belts was a Gehrig home run that opened the AL scoring.

All-Star Game:
Most games won, lifetime: 3, Vernon "Lefty" Gomez, New York (AL), 1933, 1935, 1937

Detroit's Rudy York hit 18 homers in one calendar month.

Tiger, Tiger Hitting Right

DETROIT, Michigan, August 31, 1937—Rudy York, who was sent down to the minors in June, hit his twenty-ninth and thirtieth home runs of the season today as the Tigers overpowered Washington, 12–3, at Navin Field.

For York, a rookie who played catcher today, the home runs brought his total for the month of August to 18, breaking by one Babe Ruth's mark of 17 homers in a calendar month, September, 1927, the year the Bambino hit 60.

In addition to the long blasts, both off Pete Appleton, York had two singles in a perfect 4-for-4 day. He drove in seven of the Tigers' 12 runs. Back on June 7, York, who was getting only his second chance in the big leagues after playing briefly in 1934, had been optioned on 24-hour recall to the Toledo Mud Hens of the American Association as the Tigers called up center-fielder Chet Laabs.

Most home runs in a calendar month: 18, Rudy York, Detroit (AL), August, 1937

Dutch Treat

BROOKLYN, New York, June 15, 1938—There was a festive mood at Ebbets Field as a crowd of 38,748 paid to see the first major league night baseball game in the New York metropolitan area. In the stands were about 500 people from Midland Park, New Jersey, hometown of Johnny Vander Meer, who had pitched a no-hitter five days ago for the Cincinnati Reds against the Boston Bees.

Tonight, John's parents, his Dutch uncles and aunts and friends were on hand to present him with a gift and to watch the 23-year-old fireballer pitch against the Brooklyn Dodgers. And pitch he did. For six innings, not one Dodger got on base. Then, in the seventh inning, something went wrong and Vander Meer issued consecutive walks to Cookie Lavagetto and Dolph Camilli. He escaped from the inning without giving up a hit, though, and sailed through the eighth. That was 17⅓ consecutive innings of hitless pitching, topped only by the legendary Cy Young's 23 hitless frames in 1904.

The first night game in history at Ebbets Field, in 1938, made history in more ways than one.

With the Reds comfortably ahead, 6–0, Buddy Hassett led off the home half of the last inning by tapping the ball toward the mound. Vandy picked it up and tagged the runner on his way to first. One out. Babe Phelps was up next and walked. Vandy's fastball had gone haywire, for he walked Lavagetto and Camilli again in quick succession. Bases loaded, one out. Ernie Koy came up to bat and drove a hard grounder to Lew Riggs at third. Riggs was so careful fielding the ball and getting it to catcher Ernie Lombardi for the force play that there was no time for a relay and possible double play.

The bases were still full when Leo Durocher came to the plate. A deathly silence filled Ebbets Field. Durocher swung, the crowd groaned, and a hard-hit ball curved foul into the right field stands. Durocher then lofted a short fly to centerfield which Harry Craft hauled in. Vandy had his second no-hitter in five days.

Others had pitched two no-hitters, but none had ever pitched two in one season, much less in successive games.

Most consecutive no-hitters: 2, Johnny Vander Meer, Cincinnati (NL), June 11 and June 15, 1938

Cincinnati's Johnny Vander Meer is the only man in history to pitch back-to-back no-hitters.

Red Sox slugger Jimmy Foxx heads for first on one of his six bases on balls.

Foxx Trot

ST. LOUIS, Missouri, June 16, 1938—Question: How can a batter get on base six times, score two runs, and not have a time at bat?
Answer: Ask Jimmy Foxx.

Foxx, leading the American League with 19 home runs and 71 runs batted in, was issued a base on balls in each of his six plate appearances as the Red Sox beat the St. Louis Browns, 12–8. The Boston first baseman got the passes from three St. Louis hurlers: Les Tietje, Ed Linke, and Russ Van Atta.

The six walks breaks the modern mark of five in one game

shared by Mel Ott of the New York Giants and Max Bishop of the Philadelphia Athletics. It also ties the pre-1900 mark of six walks set by Walter Wilmut of the Chicago Cubs in 1891.

The six plate appearances with no official time at bat duplicates the feat of Miller Huggins with the St. Louis Cardinals in 1910 and Bill Urbanski with the Boston Braves in 1934. These men did it with four walks and two sacrifices, while Charles Smith of Boston received five walks and was hit by a pitched ball back in 1890.

Most walks, game: 6, Jimmy Foxx, Boston (AL), June 16, 1938

Detroit's Charlie Gehringer batted .500 in All-Star competition.

All-Star Hitter

CINCINNATI, Ohio, July 6, 1938—Three National League pitchers held the American League to a lone run as the senior circuit All-Stars won the midsummer classic, 4–1, before a crowd of 27,067 in Crosley Field here today.

One of the seven hits given up by the Reds' Johnny Vander Meer, the Cubs' Bill Lee, and Pittsburgh's Mace Brown, went to Charlie Gehringer. The Detroit second baseman, who was one for three in the game, picked up his tenth All-Star hit in 20 times at bat for a record .500 batting average.

The loss, only the second in six games for the AL, was the first in All-Star competition for Vernon "Lefty" Gomez of the Yankees, who had won three of the previous encounters.

All-Star Game:
Highest batting average, (minimum 20 at-bats): .500, Charlie
*   Gehringer, Detroit (AL), 1933–38*

Yankee manager Joe McCarthy (right) let Lou Gehrig bench himself after 2,130 consecutive games.

Thank You, Mr. Pipp

DETROIT, Michigan, May 2, 1939—Batting an anemic .143 with four singles in 28 times at bat, Lou Gehrig benched himself today and thus ended the longest streak of consecutive games played in baseball history, 2,130. Gehrig was replaced by Ellsworth "Babe" Dahlgren, who hit a home run and a double as the Yankees overwhelmed the Tigers, 22–2, at Briggs Stadium.

Gehrig's decision to take himself out of the lineup was made with the approval of manager Joe McCarthy. "He'd let me go until the cows come home," Gehrig said of McCarthy. "He is that considerate of my feelings, but I knew in Sunday's game that I should get out of there." Two days ago, Gehrig was held hitless by Joe Krakauskas and Alex Carresquel as Washington beat New York, 3–2.

"It's tough to see your mates on base, have a chance to win a ball game and not be able to do anything about it," Gehrig said.

Gehrig's streak began June 1, 1925, when he was sent up to pinch-hit for shortstop PeeWee Wanninger. He failed to get a hit off Walter Johnson, but was in the Yankee starting lineup the following day when regular first baseman Wally Pipp told manager Miller Huggins, "I don't feel like getting in there."

Most consecutive games played: 2,130, Lou Gehrig, New York (AL), June 1, 1925 to April 30, 1939

Yankee Clipper Joe DiMaggio extends his batting streak to 56 games with a single against Cleveland's Al Milnar.

Streaking Clipper

CLEVELAND, Ohio, July 17, 1941—A crowd of 67,468, the largest ever to see a major league baseball game played at night, was on hand in Municipal Stadium tonight to see whether Joe Di-Maggio could extend his all-time record consecutive-game hitting streak.

The Yankee Clipper hit in his fifty-sixth straight game yesterday when he smashed Al Milnar's first pitch to him in the first inning through the box for a single. DiMaggio added another single and a double in New York's 10–3 victory over the Indians.

The hitting streak began May 15 in Yankee Stadium in New York when Joltin' Joe went one-for-four against the White Sox. When the skein hit 45, DiMaggio eclipsed the former record of 44 set by Wee Willie Keeler of the Baltimore Orioles in 1897.

DiMaggio, who hit in 61 straight games playing in his native San Francisco with the Seals in the Pacific Coast League eight years ago, made four trips to the plate tonight. In the first inning he hit a hard smash that third baseman Ken Keltner knocked down and threw to first in time to get DiMaggio. The next time up Joe walked. After that he hit another drive that Keltner handled.

The bases were full in the eighth when DiMaggio came up to face righthanded Jim Bagby, pitching in relief of lefty Al Smith. DiMag hit a 1-1 pitch on the ground and the hit was turned into a double play that ended the inning as well as his batting streak. The Yankees won, 4–3, but DiMaggio's streak was stopped after 56 games.

Most consecutive games one or more hits: 56, Joe DiMaggio, New York (AL), May 15, 1941 to July 16, 1941

Indian Courage

CLEVELAND, Ohio, July 13, 1954—Al Rosen told American League manager Casey Stengel before today's All-Star Game that he was willing to be dropped from the starting lineup, selected by a poll of the fans. Rosen broke a finger May 25 and the injury had been affecting his performance, but Stengel left the Cleveland infielder in the order, batting fifth and playing first base. Rosen responded by leading the AL to a 11–9 victory, giving Stengel his first victory as an All-Star manager over rookie NL pilot, Walter Alston of the Brooklyn Dodgers.

Playing before a crowd of 68,751 in Municipal Stadium, three Indians treated the hometown fans to outstanding performances. Rosen hit two home runs and drove in five runs, Larry Doby clouted a pinch-hit home run and Bobby Avila went three-for-three and scored a run. Rosen's five runs batted in tied an All-Star record set by Ted Williams in 1946, and his two homers equaled the efforts of Williams and Pittsburgh's Arky Vaughn in 1941. Despite the bum finger, Rosen played the entire game, eight innings at first before moving to third base, replacing Detroit's Ray Boone, whose homer had provided the margin of victory for the junior circuit.

All-Star Game:
Most runs batted in, game: 5, Al Rosen, Cleveland (AL), July 13, 1954 (Ties Ted Williams, Boston (AL), July 9, 1946)

Special Delivery

NEW YORK, October 8, 1956—Using a no-windup delivery, Don Larsen of the New York Yankees retired 27 Brooklyn Dodger batters in succession today as he pitched the only perfect game in World Series history. There had never even been a no-hitter in the Series, much less a perfect game.

The scoreboard tells it all in Don Larsen's perfect game against the Dodgers.

The 27-year-old righthander, a native of Michigan City, Indiana, who grew up in San Diego, California, retired the final batter, pinch-hitter Dale Mitchell, with a fastball that was called strike three by umpire Babe Pinelli. The Yankees won, 2–0.

Crediting his unusual pitching motion, which is a modification of the stretch pitchers normally use with runners on base, Larsen said after the game, "It gives me better control, it takes nothing off my fastball, and it keeps the batters tense. They have to be ready every second."

There were only four near-hits Dodger batters could manage against the 6-foot 4-inch, 220-pound Larsen, who won only three games while losing 21 two seasons ago before being traded from Baltimore to the Yanks. In the second inning, third baseman Andy Carey got his glove in the way of a liner off the bat of Jackie Robinson. The ball bounced to shortstop Gil MacDougald and he pegged to first in time to nip the fleet Robinson.

In the fifth inning, Mickey Mantle made a spectacular catch in deep left center on a clout by Gil Hodges. The next batter, Sandy Amoros, hit a long drive down the rightfield line that curved foul just before going into the stands. And in the eighth inning, it was Hodges again who almost ruined Larsen's effort when he hit a low smash down the third base line. Carey made a diving stab, but just to make sure he wasn't called for trapping it, Carey threw to first baseman Joe Collins for an unnecessary putout.

World Series:
Most consecutive batters retired, game: 27, Don Larsen, New York (AL), vs. Brooklyn (NL), October 8, 1956

Splendid Splinter

WASHINGTON, D.C., July 10, 1956—Boston's Ted Williams and the New York Yankees' Mickey Mantle socked consecutive home runs and knocked Warren Spahn out of the box, but it still was not enough to bring victory to the American League today, as the National League won, 7–3, for the sixth time in the last seven All-Star Games.

Williams, the Splendid Splinter who has been playing in these midsummer classics since 1940 when he hasn't been fighting in wars, homered with Chicago's Nellie Fox on base. It was Williams' first home run in 10 years. His last came in 1946 when he had a pair at Fenway Park in Boston. But the runs batted in today increased his total in All-Star Games to a record 12.

The Red Sox' Ted Williams holds the All-Star Game mark of 12 runs batted in.

All-Star Game:
Most runs batted in, career: 12, Ted Williams, Boston (AL), 1940–
    56

Pittsburgh's Harvey Haddix retired 36 batters in a row in one game, and lost.

12/13ths Perfect

MILWAUKEE, Wisconsin, May 26, 1959—A perfect game that wasn't and a home run that was a double spelled victory for the Milwaukee Braves tonight. Pittsburgh's Harvey "The Kitten" Haddix stymied the heavy-hitting Braves, retiring a record 36 consecutive batters in 12 innings. And although Milwaukee's Lew Burdette gave up 12 hits, the Pirates failed to score in their 13 turns at bat.

Haddix, who struck out eight Braves, started the bottom of the thirteenth facing Felix Mantilla, who was safe on an error by third baseman Don Hoak. Haddix' perfect game was gone, but it was still better than the 33 consecutive batters retired by Brooklyn's Ed Kimber against Toledo in 1884, back when the American Association was a major league. And even if the Kitten's perfect game was ruined, he still had his no-hitter.

Eddie Mathews sacrificed Mantilla to second. Henry Aaron, leading the majors with a .442 batting average, was walked intentionally. This pitted lefthanded Haddix against righthanded batter Joe Adcock. The big Louisianan teed off on Haddix and parked the ball over the right center field fence. Haddix was dejected, Adcock elated with the home run and the Braves' 3-0 victory, until Frank Dascoli changed the scoring. The umpire said that Aaron, who had cut across the infield after touching second base, had been passed on the baselines by Adcock, so Adcock was out. Aaron then went back, retraced his steps from second, touched third and home to score. He and Mantilla had scored the runs and the Braves won, 2-0. Adcock was given credit for a double. Haddix lost the perfect game, the no-hitter, and picked up a spectacular one-hit loss.

Most consecutive batters retired, game: 36, Harvey Haddix, Pittsburgh (NL), May 26, 1959

Men for All Ages

NEW YORK, July 13, 1960—One man many people consider too young was nominated for one job while another man who is called too old by some got a different job done today.

In Los Angeles, 43-year-old John F. Kennedy won the Democratic nomination for President, while here in Yankee Stadium 39-year-old Stan Musial hit a record sixth home run in All-Star competition to help the National League to a 6-0 victory.

Musial, who laced a pinch-hit single in this year's first All-Star Game, which the NL won, 5-3, in Kansas City two days ago, appeared again in a pinch-hitting role in the second All-Star Game of 1960. Playing in his nineteenth classic, Stan the Man came up in the fourth inning to bat for pitcher Stan Williams and knocked a solo blast off Gerry Staley for the National's fourth run. All of the runs were scored via homers, one each by San Francisco's Willie

The Cardinals' Stan Musial (far left), who set the All-Star mark of six home runs, celebrates with Willie Mays, Vernon Law, Eddie Mathews and Ken Boyer.

Mays, Milwaukee's Eddie Mathews, and Musial's Cardinal teammate, Ken Boyer.

Another old-timer who was roundly cheered by the crowd was Ted Williams, six weeks short of his 42nd birthday, who singled in a pinch-hitting role for the AL.

All-Star Game
Most home runs, career: 6, Stan Musial, St. Louis,(NL) 1948–60

Driving Them In

PITTSBURGH, Pennsylvania, October 12, 1960—Yankee second baseman Bobby Richardson—described by sportswriters as too good to be true—was almost too good to be believed again today as he touched Pirate pitchers for a pair of triples, drove in three runs, earned another line in the record book and, incidentally, helped New York to a 12–0 World Series triumph.

Richardson, a native of South Carolina who doesn't smoke, drink, or cuss, set a single-game record with six runs batted in during the third game of the Series, won by the Yankees, 10–0. The 25-year-old, 5-foot 9-inch and 165-pound Richardson slammed a bases-loaded home run in the first inning of that game, went four-for-four at the plate and drove in two more runs to eclipse the mark of five RBIs shared by Yankees Bill Dickey and Tony Lazzeri, set in 1936 and equaled by Mickey Mantle in the opening game of this series.

Today, Richardson tripled in the third inning off Tom Cheney to drive in Johnny Blanchard and Yogi Berra. These were his tenth and eleventh runs batted in, surpassing the 10 RBIs by Berra in 1956 and duplicated by Ted Kluszewski of the White Sox in last year's series. Bobby upped the record to 12 when he tripled again in the seventh inning off Clem Labine, scoring Blanchard.

World Series:
Most runs batted in, series: 12, Bobby Richardson, New York (AL), 1960
Most runs batted in, game: 6, Bobby Richardson, New York (AL), October 8, 1960

Say Hey, Four Times

MILWAUKEE, Wisconsin, April 30, 1961—Willie Mays became the ninth player in major league history to hit four home runs in one game as he cleared the fences in County Stadium in the first, third, sixth, and eighth innings today in San Francisco's 14-4 rout of the Milwaukee Braves.

With the slim Sunday afternoon crowd of 13,114 rooting him on, Mays reached the on-deck circle in the ninth inning but Jim Davenport's ground out prevented the Say Hey Kid from trying for No. 5. Mays came into the game in a slump, having failed to hit in seven tries in the first two games of the series, which included a no-hitter by the Braves' Warren Spahn Friday night.

In what he described as "easily the greatest day I've ever had," Mays hit two homers off starter Lew Burdette, one off Seth Morehead, and one off Don McMahon. Only Moe Drabowsky, in the fifth, was able to retire Mays, who drove in eight runs with his four blasts.

With Jose Pagan hitting a pair of homers and one each for Orlando Cepeda and Felipe Alou, the Giants tied the major league record with eight home runs in the game. San Francisco, with five round-trippers in yesterday's game, also tied the 1939 Yankee record of 13 homers in two consecutive games.

Most home runs, game: 4, Willie Mays, San Francisco (NL), April 30, 1961 (Ties Robert L. Lowe, Boston (NL), May 30, 1894; Edward Delahanty, Philadelphia (NL), July 13, 1896; Lou Gehrig,

New York (AL), June 3, 1932; Chuck Klein, Philadelphia (NL), July 10, 1936; J. Patrick Seery, Chicago (AL), July 18, 1948; Gil Hodges, Brooklyn (NL), August 31, 1950; Joseph Adcock, Milwaukee (NL), July 31, 1954; Rocky Colavito, Cleveland (AL), June 10, 1959)

Most home runs, team, two consecutive games: 8, San Francisco (NL), April 29–30, 1961 (Ties New York (AL), June 28, 1939, doubleheader)

San Francisco's Willie Mays crosses the plate after hitting his fourth home run against Milwaukee.

One Up on the Babe

NEW YORK, October 1, 1961—The record that many people didn't want to see broken was broken today as New York's Roger Maris hit his sixty-first home run in the final game of the season off Boston Red Sox rookie Tracy Stallard. It was the 27-year-old

Yankee Roger Maris belts his sixty-first homer against the Red Sox.

lefthanded batter's forty-ninth home run off a righthanded pitcher and his thirtieth in Yankee Stadium as he pulled a waist-high fastball on a two-strike count over the right field fence in the fourth inning.

Earlier in the season, baseball Commissioner Ford Frick said if Maris were to break Babe Ruth's record of 60 home runs—the

Babe hit his sixtieth on the final day of the 1927 season—it would be noted in the record book with an asterisk. Frick said the difference was that Ruth played a 154-game schedule while Maris' Yankees had a 162-game schedule. Nevertheless, the two home run hitters had almost the same number of plate appearances in their record-breaking seasons, Ruth 692 and Maris 698. After 154 games this season, Maris had hit 59 home runs.

A crowd of 23,154 was on hand to see Maris, a native of Raytown, Missouri, give the Yankees a 1-0 victory over Boston.

Most home runs, season: 61, Roger Maris, New York (AL), 1961

Yogi's String

LOS ANGELES, California, October 5, 1963—Lawrence Peter Berra had as much trouble hitting Don Drysdale as did his Yankee teammates and as a result the Los Angeles Dodgers won their third straight World Series game today, 1-0.

Berra, who has carried his childhood nickname of Yogi throughout his baseball life, was sent up to pinch-hit for pitcher Jim Bouton. Berra failed to get a hit, but his appearance extended many of his World Series records. This marked the fourteenth time Yogi has been in a World Series, all with the Yankees. In 75 games, he has had 259 times at bat, with 71 hits, 49 of them singles, all record totals. In addition, Berra has handled more chances and completed more putouts than any fielder at any position in World Series history.

World Series:
Most World Series: 14, L.P. "Yogi" Berra, New York (AL), 1949–53, 1955–58, 1960–63
Most games: 75, L.P. "Yogi" Berra, New York (AL), 1949–53, 1955–58, 1960–63
Most times at bat: 259, L.P. "Yogi" Berra, New York (AL), 1949–53, 1955–58, 1960–63
Most hits: 71, L.P. "Yogi" Berra, New York (AL), 1949–53, 1955–58, 1960–63
Most singles: 49, L.P. "Yogi" Berra, New York (AL), 1949–53, 1955–58, 1960–63
Most chances accepted: 466, L.P. "Yogi" Berra, New York (AL), 1949–53, 1955–58, 1960–63
Most putouts: 439, L.P. "Yogi" Berra, New York (AL), 1949–53, 1955–58, 1960–63

New York's Yogi Berra pinch-hits against the Dodgers in his 259th World Series at bat.

Changing of the Guard

ST. LOUIS, Missouri, October 15, 1964—Upheavals were the order of the day today. On the banks of the Moscow River a couple of guys named Brezhnev and Kosygin toppled Nikita Khrushchev from power in the Soviet Union. And on the banks of the Mississippi, a couple of guys named Gibson and Brock ended the World Series' reign of Mickey Mantle, Whitey Ford, and the New York Yankees.

With Bob Gibson pitching and Lou Brock hitting and stealing bases, the St. Louis Cardinals beat New York, 7–5, in the seventh and final game of the World Series here today. The game marked the last post-season appearances of Ford, a part-time pitching coach, who developed a sore arm in losing the opening game of the Series, and Mantle, who hit three home runs, scored eight runs, drove in eight runs, and batted .333 for the Series. Between them, they accounted for numerous records.

It was the second successive World Series loss for the Yankees. Only in 1921 and 1922, in their first two Series appearances ever,

The New York Yankees' Mickey Mantle (below) and Whitey Ford own many World Series records.

had the Yankees lost twice in a row. In between, they won 20 of the 25 Series in which they appeared.

World Series:
Most runs, career: 42, Mickey Mantle, New York (AL), 1951–53; 1955–58; 1960–64
Most extra base hits, career: 26, Mickey Mantle, New York (AL), 1951–53; 1955–58; 1960–64
Most total bases, career: 123, Mickey Mantle, New York (AL), 1951–53; 1955–58; 1960–64
Most home runs, career: 18, Mickey Mantle, New York (AL), 1951–53; 1955–58; 1960–64
Most runs batted in, career: 40, Mickey Mantle, New York (AL), 1951–53; 1955–58; 1960–64
Most walks, career; 43, Mickey Mantle, New York (AL), 1951–53; 1955–58; 1960–64
Most strikeouts, career: 54, Mickey Mantle, New York (AL), 1951–53; 1955–58, 1960–64

World Series, pitcher:
Most series: 11, Edward C. "Whitey" Ford, New York (AL), 1950, 1953, 1955–58, 1960–64
Most games, career: 22, E.C. "Whitey" Ford, New York (AL), 1950, 1953, 1955–58, 1960–64
Most games started, career: 22, E.C. "Whitey" Ford, New York (AL), 1950, 1953, 1955–58, 1960–64
Most games won, career: 10, E.C. "Whitey" Ford, New York (AL), 1950, 1953, 1955–58, 1960–64
Most games lost, career: 8, E.C. "Whitey" Ford, New York (AL), 1950, 1953, 1955–58, 1960–64
Most innings pitched, career: 146, E.C. "Whitey" Ford, New York (AL), 1950, 1953, 1955–58, 1960–64
Most runs allowed; career: 51, E.C. "Whitey" Ford, New York (AL), 1950, 1953, 1955–58, 1960–64
Most earned runs allowed, career: 44, E.C. "Whitey" Ford, New York (AL), 1950, 1953, 1955–58, 1960–64
Most hits, career: 132, E.C. "Whitey" Ford, New York (AL), 1950, 1953, 1955–58, 1960–64
Most bases on balls, career: 34, E.C. "Whitey" Ford, New York (AL), 1950, 1953, 1955–58, 1960–64
Most strikeouts, career: 94, E.C. "Whitey" Ford, New York (AL), 1950, 1953, 1955–58, 1960–64

The Los Angeles Dodgers' Sandy Koufax throws his perfect game against the Chicago Cubs.

Hitting the Wind

LOS ANGELES, California, September 9, 1965—A pair of lefthanders locked horns in a pitching duel and the result was very nearly a double no-hitter. Pitching for the hometown Dodgers was Sandy Koufax, with a flashy 21–7 record and the league lead in strikeouts with 318. Going for the Chicago Cubs was well-traveled Bob Hendley, sporting a 2-win, 2-loss record.

Batters were helpless against the portsiders, failing to reach base for four innings. Then, in the bottom of the fifth, Lou Johnson worked Hendley for a walk, to become the first base runner of the game. Ron Fairly sacrificed. Then Johnson stole third and, when catcher Chris Krug pegged the ball into left field, went home to score. Hendley lost the perfect game, the shutout and the lead, but still had his no-hitter intact. Koufax, meanwhile, was crafting a perfect game.

The pressure was mounting and in the seventh inning, it was Johnson, again, who figured in the play. With two out, he blooped a double down the left field line. He was left stranded, the only man to be left on base during the entire game.

Koufax, in the next half-inning, decided to cut things as short as possible and proceeded to strike out Ron Santo, Ernie Banks, and rookie Byron Browne. He ended the game the following inning by whiffing the erring Krug, and pinch-hitters Joey Amalfitano and Harvey Kuenn. The perfect game, with 14 strikeouts, was a record fourth no-hitter for Koufax, one more than the number pitched by Cy Young, Bob Feller and Larry Corcoran.

Most no-hitters, career: 4, Sandy Koufax, Brooklyn (NL), and Los Angeles (NL), 1955–66
Fewest hits, both teams, one game: 1, Chicago (0) and Los Angeles (1), National League, September 9, 1965

MOE-ing Them Down

LOS ANGELES, California, October 5, 1966—Moe Drabowsky, who shares the American League record of hitting four batters in one game, pitched his way into the record books again today. Hurling for the Baltimore Orioles against the Los Angeles Dodgers in the World Series opener, Drabowsky came on in relief of Dave McNally in the third inning.

He struck out Wes Parker, forced in a run by walking Jim Gilliam and then retired John Roseboro to quell a Dodger uprising. Drabowsky fanned a record 11 batters in all, allowed only one hit and protected the Orioles' lead as Baltimore went on to win, 5-2.

Cast off earlier this season by Kansas City, Drabowsky started the fourth inning today by striking out pinch-hitter Jim Barbieri. Maury Wills and Willie Davis were also retired via the strikeout route. The 31-year-old Drabowsky, born in Ozanna, Poland, then proceeded to fan three more Dodgers in the fifth—Lou Johnson, Tommy Davis, and Jim Lefebvre—to tie the record of six straight set by Cincinnati's Hod Eller against the White Sox in the scandal-tainted series of 1919. The 11 strikeouts by Drabowsky, a record total for a relief pitcher, bettered the mark of 10 by Jess Barnes of the Giants against the Yankees in 1921.

Drabowsky's four hit batsmen came in a regular season game when he was pitching for the Chicago White Sox, June 2, 1957.

World Series:
Most consecutive strikeouts: 6, Myron W. "Moe" Drabowsky, Baltimore (AL), October 5, 1966
Most strikeouts by a relief pitcher: 11, Myron W. "Moe" Drabowsky, Baltimore (AL), October 5, 1966

Baltimore's Moe Drabowsky makes Dodger Jim Lefebvre his sixth consecutive strikeout victim.

Chicago Cub Fergie Jenkins ties Carl Hubbell, Johnny Vander Meer and Larry Jansen with six strikeouts in All-Star Game.

Pitcher Power

ANAHEIM, California, July 11, 1967—The pitchers overpowered the hitters, and so the All-Star Game continued for a record 15 innings today until Cincinnati's Tony Perez blasted a home run off

Oakland's Jim "Catfish" Hunter to give the Nationals a 2–1 triumph. All the runs were scored on homers, one by the Phillies' Dick Allen off Minnesota's Dean Chance in the second inning, and a sixth-inning blast by Baltimore's Brooks Robinson off Ferguson Jenkins.

In between the home runs, it was all pitchers. Every hurler struck out at least one batter, with Chicago's Jenkins getting a record-tying six. When New York Met rookie Tom Seaver whiffed Ken Berry to end the game, it was the thirtieth strikeout of the contest, 10 over the old two-team record. In addition, Pittsburgh's two-time batting champion Roberto Clemente also entered the record books by being a four-time strikeout victim of Chance, Hunter, Gary Peters and Al Downing.

Jenkins, in equaling the statistics of Carl Hubbell, Johnny Vander Meer and Larry Jansen, struck out Harmon Killebrew, Tony Conigliaro, Mickey Mantle, Jim Fregosi, Rod Carew, and Tony Oliva.

All-Star Game:
Most strikeouts by a pitcher: 6, Ferguson Jenkins, Chicago (AL), 1967 (Ties Carl Hubbell, New York (NL), 1934; Johnny Vander Meer, Cincinnati (NL), 1943; Larry Jansen, New York (NL), 1950)
Most strikeouts by a batter: 4, Roberto Clemente, Pittsburgh (NL), July 11, 1967

A Long Time Coming

HOUSTON, Texas, April 16, 1968—How long can a team go without scoring a run in one game? Houston gave the New York Mets 24 innings tonight before the Astros scored a run in the Astrodome to end the longest one-run shutout in baseball history.

Since the game began on April 15—the day income taxes are due—it may not be surprising that the Mets came up empty. The victory didn't exactly cover the Astros with glory, though.

Here's how the winning run was scored: Norm Miller walked in the bottom of the twenty-fourth inning and advanced to second base on a balk by Met pitcher Les Rohr. Jim Wynn was walked intentionally. Then Rusty Staub moved the runners to second and third on a ground out. Another intentional walk, to Hal King, loaded the bases. Houston's Bob Aspromonte then hit what

The Mets' Tom Seaver toils against Houston in the longest 1-0 game in history.

looked like a double play ball, but Met shortstop Al Weis turned it into a run-scoring bobble.

Longest 1–0 game: 24 innings, New York Mets vs. Houston (NL), April 15–16, 1968

Longest game with no outfield assists: New York Mets vs. Houston (NL), April 15–16, 1968

Most innings caught, game: 24, Hal King, Houston (NL) and Jerry Grote, New York Mets (NL), April 15, 1968

The Dodgers' Don Drysdale pitched more All-Star Game innings than anyone else.

Dandy Don

HOUSTON, Texas, July 9, 1968—Willie Mays of the San Francisco Giants scored an unearned run in the first inning, but it was enough to provide the National League with a 1–0 victory and give Don Drysdale his second straight All-Star Game decision.

Starting for the fifth time in eight All-Star Games, Drysdale extended his record appearance to 19⅓ innings and although he failed to fan anyone today, retained his career record of 19 strikeouts in All-Star competition.

Before the Los Angeles Dodger star displayed his mound mastery in the Astrodome, Drysdale learned that one of his regular season records had been revised. Earlier this season he had pitched a record six straight shutouts and 58⅔ scoreless innings. Today, however, the Baseball Writers Association, custodian of baseball records, said it would consider only whole innings in the record. So Drysdale will be credited with only 58 shutout innings, two more than the former record of 56 pitched by Walter Johnson in 1913.

All-Star Game:
Most innings pitched: 19⅓, Don Drysdale, Los Angeles (NL), 1959–68
Most strikeouts: 19, Don Drysdale, Los Angeles (NL), 1959–68

All Over the Field

BLOOMINGTON, Minnesota, September 22, 1968—Minnesota starting pitcher Cesar Tovar gave up no hits or runs, struck out one batter, walked one, and committed a balk in the first inning of tonight's game against the Oakland A's. Tovar, normally a shortstop, proceeded to play a different position each inning after that as the Twins beat Oakland, 2–1.

The first batter that Tovar faced on the mound was Bert Campaneris, who is the only other man to play all nine positions in a single major league game. He did it with the A's in Kansas City three seasons ago.

In addition to his pitching and errorless fielding, Tovar had one hit and scored a run in the Twins' triumph.

Minnesota's Cesar Tovar tied a record when he played all nine positions in one game.

Gibby's ERA

ST. LOUIS, Missouri, September 26, 1968—St. Louis ace Bob Gibson hurled a six-hit shutout tonight en route to compiling the lowest earned-run average in major league history. The Cardinal righthander blanked the Houston Astros, 1-0, for his thirteenth shutout of the season and an ERA of 1.12. Gibson's mark betters the 51-year-old record of 1.22 set by Grover Cleveland Alexander in 1917.

Curt Flood drove in Mike Shannon in the home half of the fifth inning to provide Gibson with the only run he needed, as he struck out 11 Astros to raise his league-leading total to 268. The victory was number 22, against nine losses for Gibby as the World Series-bound Cardinals played before a crowd of 18,658.

Bob Gibson of the St. Louis Cardinals has the record for lowest earned-run average in a season.

Lowest earned-run average, season (minimum 300 innings pitched): 1.12, Bob Gibson, St. Louis (NL), 1968

Striking a Losing Pose

ST. LOUIS, Missouri, October 10, 1968—The Detroit Tigers captured the World Series by winning their third straight game today, 4–1, and not even strikeout king Bob Gibson could prevent it.

Gibson, who fanned a record 17 batters in the Series opener, struck out eight Tigers today in upping his World Series record total to 35. But in the end it was a game-winning rally that produced three runs in the seventh inning and gave Mickey Lolich his third victory of the Series and the Tigers the world championship.

World Series:
Most strikeouts, series: 35, Bob Gibson, St. Louis (NL), 1968
Most strikeouts, game: 17, Bob Gibson, St. Louis (NL), vs. Detroit, October 2, 1968
Most victories, series: 3, Mickey Lolich, Detroit Tigers (AL), 1968 (Ties Christy Mathewson, New York (NL), 1905; Charles "Babe" Adams, Pittsburgh (NL), 1909; Jack Coombs, Philadel-

Detroit's Mickey Lolich won three games in a single World Series against the Cardinals.

phia (AL), 1910; Urban Faber, Chicago (AL), 1917; Stan Covel-eski, Cleveland (AL), 1920; Harry Brecheen, St. Louis (NL), 1946; Lou Burdette, Milwaukee (NL), 1957; Bob Gibson, St. Louis (NL), 1967)

Boston's Carl Yastrzemski shares the record for most hits in an All-Star Game.

Night All-Stars

CINCINNATI, Ohio, July 14, 1970—Despite a bi-partisan start by President Richard Nixon, the first night All-Star Game ever played was an all-National League affair in Cincinnati's new Riverfront Stadium. Nixon, attending the game with daughter Julie and her husband, David Eisenhower, threw out two "first balls"—one to Cincinnati catcher Johnny Bench and one to AL starting receiver Bill Freehan of Detroit.

The Nationals scored three runs in the ninth inning and one in the twelfth to defeat the Americans, 5–4, winning their eighth straight classic and their twelfth in the last 13 games. The lone bright spot in the AL firmament was Boston's Carl Yastrzemski, who rapped three singles and a double in earning Most Valuable Player honors, the only thing the AL has won recently. The four hits by Yaz ties the number hit by Ducky Medwick in the 1937 game and matched by Ted Williams of the Red Sox at Fenway Park in 1946.

In bringing night All-Star baseball to the city where nighttime play was introduced to the big leagues, the Nationals won their sixth extra inning game in six tries. The winning run scored on successive singles by the Reds' Pete Rose, Los Angeles' Billy Grabar-kowitz and Chicago's Jim Hickman.

All-Star Game:
Most hits, one game: 4, Carl Yastrzemski, Boston (AL), 1970 (Ties Joseph Medwick, St. Louis (NL), 1937; Ted Williams, Boston (AL), 1946)

Mob Scene

OAKLAND, California, September 19, 1972—The Chicago White Sox and Oakland A's, separated by three games in the American League West standings, used a record 51 players in a 15-inning, 4-hour and 51-minute game finally won by Chicago, 8-7.

With rosters swollen by minor leaguers called up after the September expansion date, the A's used 30 players—a record for one team—including seven pitchers, eight pinch-hitters and a pinch-runner. Oakland manager Dick Williams also used five different second basemen: Dal Maxvil, Ted Kubiak, Dick Green, Tim Cullen, and Larry Haney.

Chicago manager Chuck Tanner had the last laugh, though, when Jorge Ortega—who had come in to play second base in the eighth inning as a defensive replacement for Mike Andrews—hit his second home run of the year to win the game in the fifteenth inning.

Most players used, one team, game: 30, Oakland vs. Chicago (AL), September 19, 1972
Most players used, both teams, game: 51, Oakland (30) and Chicago (21) (AL), September 19, 1972

Gene Who?

OAKLAND, California, October 20, 1972—This season continues to be one of the strangest in baseball annals. To start with, the season almost didn't. The opening was delayed because of a players' strike. Then the Mustache Gang, as the hirsute Oakland A's are called, won the American League pennant. The last time the Athletics appeared in the World Series was in 1931, when Connie

Oakland's Gene Tenace hit four home runs against Cincinnati in a World Series.

Mack ran the team in Philadelphia before it shifted to Kansas City en route to Oakland.

And today, Cincinnati won, 5-4, but it was Oakland catcher Gene Tenace who will have his name in the record book alongside Babe Ruth, Lou Gehrig, Duke Snider, and Hank Bauer as men who have hit four home runs in a single Series.

Tenace knocked two round trippers opening day off Gary Nolan, and hit another in the fourth game, each won by Oakland with the identical score of 3-2. In today's loss, Tenace smashed his three-run blast off Jim McGlothin to give the A's a lead they couldn't hold.

World Series:
Most home runs, one series: 4, Gene Tenace, Oakland (AL), 1972
(Ties George H. "Babe" Ruth, New York (AL), 1926; Lou Gehrig, New York (AL), 1928; Edwin "Duke" Snider, Brooklyn (NL), 1952 and 1955; Henry Bauer, New York (AL), 1958)

Say Hey, One More Time

KANSAS CITY, Missouri, July 24, 1973—It took a special ruling from Commissioner Bowie Kuhn to do it, but Willie Mays played in a record-tying twenty-fourth All-Star Game. Kuhn increased the player limit for the game so that stars such as Mays and California's no-hit pitcher Nolan Ryan could be included on the All-Star rosters. As a result, there were a record 58 players selected for the squads, 54 of whom saw action in the National League's 7–1 victory in Royals Stadium, part of the new Harry S. Truman Sports Complex here.

Home runs by Cincinnati's Johnny Bench, San Francisco's Bobby Bonds, and Los Angeles' Willie Davis powered the NL to its tenth triumph in the last 11 games.

Mays, whose first 23 appearances were in a Giant uniform, was representing the New York Mets this year. And even though he was struck out by the Yankees' Sparky Lyle, who was in his first All-Star Game, Mays received a standing ovation from the crowd of 40,849.

All-Star Game:

Most games: 24, Willie Mays, New York (NL), San Francisco (NL), New York (NL), 1951–73, (Ties Stan Musial, St. Louis (NL), 1943–63)

Most times on winning team: 17, Willie Mays, National League

Most at bats: 75, Willie Mays, New York (NL), San Francisco (NL), New York (NL), 1951–73

Most runs: 20, Willie Mays, New York (NL), San Francisco (NL), New York (NL), 1951–73

Most hits: 23, Willie Mays, New York (NL), San Francisco (NL), New York (NL), 1951–73

Most singles: 15, Willie Mays, New York (NL), San Francisco (NL), New York (NL), 1951–73

Most extra base hits: 8, Willie Mays, New York (NL), San Francisco (NL), New York (NL), 1951–73

Most stolen bases: 6, Willie Mays, New York (NL), San Francisco (NL), New York (NL), 1951–73

Alone at the Top

ATLANTA, Georgia, April 8, 1974—The Dodger pitcher went into his stretch, looked the runner back to first base, drew back,

Henry Aaron has hit more home runs than anyone in history.

and fired home. The ball was straight and true, over the plate and rising slightly along the way. The batter swung hard, unleashing power with a last instant snap of the wrists. The ball sailed toward the left field fence.

Henry Aaron slowed to a trot rounding first base after he had watched the ball elude the flailing reach of Bill Buckner, who had scaled the fence to lunge at the ball. The crowd was hammering, hooting, stomping, and whistling approval. Two teen-age boys joined Aaron on his circuit of the bases. Dodger infielders congratulated him as he went by.

This was the 715th time Henry Aaron had hit a home run in a regular season major league game. This was the blast that moved Aaron to the top of the heap, ahead of Babe Ruth, as the all-time leading hitter of home runs. The event had been anticipated for nearly a year, all the plans had been made, festivities scheduled, awards designed. Only the date could not be predetermined. Television was there, with an unusual Monday night game early in the season being beamed nationally. Baseball Commissioner Bowie Kuhn was noticeably absent, since he had unpopularly dictated that Aaron must play in two games in Cincinnati before the Braves played their home opener in Atlanta Stadium tonight. And 52,780 people were in Atlanta Stadium in the hope of watching history in the making.

It came to pass in the fourth inning, as Aaron came up to bat, carrying a 34-ounce Del Crandell model Louisville Slugger. The Dodgers were leading, 3-1, and Darrell Evans was on first base. The pitcher was Al Downing, who like Aaron wore uniform No. 44. Downing's first pitch was a ball, outside. The next pitch was the home run everyone had come to see.

Few people remember Aaron's first home run, hit in 1954 off Vic Raschi, or many in-between, although there were important ones like the clout in 1957 that brought Milwaukee its first pennant when the Braves called County Stadium home.

And there are those individuals who don't believe Aaron's record is tops, citing Ruth's era of the "dead ball" and fewer games and times at bat. But these are the same individuals who forget Aaron's night games, coast-to-coast plane trips, and generally poor supporting cast.

The story is in the numbers, and these say Aaron is the greatest home run hitter of all time.

Most home runs, career: 733*, Henry Aaron, Milwaukee (NL), 1954-65; Atlanta, (NL), 1966-74; Milwaukee (AL), 1975

*As of start of 1975 season

Nolan Ryan's 19 K's

ANAHEIM, California, August 12, 1974—Nolan Ryan has seen every 19-strikeout performance that has occurred in the major leagues in modern times. Tonight, his striking out 19 Red Sox in nine innings broke Bob Feller's American League record and tied

California's Nolan Ryan struck out 19 batters in a nine-inning game.

the major league mark, as the California Angels beat Boston, 4–2.

Ryan was there on the New York Met bench when Steve Carlton, pitching for the St. Louis Cardinals, struck out 19 Mets on September 15, 1969. Carlton lost that game when Ron Swoboda hit two home runs and helped the Mets to a pennant.

Ryan was on the bench again when Met teammate Tom Seaver struck out 19 San Diego Padres—including a record 10 consecutive—on April 22, 1970.

Ryan himself struck out 19 batters, against this same Red Sox team earlier this year, on June 15. But those came in a 15-inning game and didn't set any records, since Tom Cheney of the old Washington Senators had struck out 21 Baltimore Orioles in a 16-inning game on September 12, 1962.

But tonight it was Ryan's turn for the record book, as he moved his fast ball over, under and around the bats of the Boston hitters. Sixteen of the 19 strikeout victims went down swinging. The 19th strikeout of the game, and the one that snapped Feller's record of 18 set in 1938, came in the ninth inning on a 3-2 pitch to Bernie Carbo. Ryan had one chance for a record-shattering 20th K. But Rick Burleson proved elusive. He was the only Boston starter Ryan failed to whiff all night, and he ended the game by hitting a two-strike pitch to left field, where it was hauled in by Bruce Bochte, for the final out.

Most batters struck out, nine innings: 19, Nolan Ryan, California (AL), vs. Boston, August 12, 1974 (Ties Steve Carlton, St. Louis (NL), vs. New York Mets, September 15, 1969; Tom Seaver, New York Mets (NL), vs. San Diego, April 22, 1970)

In the Wee Small Hours

NEW YORK, September 13, 1974—It took two errors to do it, but the St. Louis Cardinals finally managed to beat the New York Mets, 4–3, after 25 innings, seven hours and four minutes of baseball in Shea Stadium which began last night and ended early this morning.

The only longer game played was the May 1, 1920 affair in which the Boston Braves and Brooklyn Dodgers couldn't decide on a winner after 26 innings of play and so the game was called on account of darkness with the score tied, 1–1.

The Mets thought they had the game won in regulation time, leading 3–1 with two out and one man on in the ninth inning. But Ken Rietz hit a home run and the decision was postponed 16 innings.

The Cardinals scored the winning run on Bake McBride's infield hit and a throwing error by Met pitcher Hank Webb. With McBride leading off first following his hit, Webb tried to pick him off and sailed the ball past first baseman John Milner. McBride took off around the bases as Milner took off after the ball. By the time the Met first baseman picked up the ball, McBride was heading for home. The throw from Milner was true, but catcher Ron Hodges dropped it as McBride came sliding in safe. Webb and Hodges were given errors.

Longest night game: 25 innings, St. Louis vs. New York Mets (NL), September 12, 1974
Longest game played to a decision: 25 innings, St. Louis 4, New York Mets 3 (NL), September 12, 1974

Striking Angel

ANAHEIM, California, September 28, 1974—Record-setting Nolan Ryan and his smoking fastball ended the season in spectacular fashion tonight as Ryan pitched the third no-hitter of his career in California's 4–0 victory over Minnesota.

Ryan struck out 15 Twins, raising his season total to 367, to go with his major league record of 383 strikeouts last year and 329 in 1972. The designated hitter—who bats in place of the pitcher—was introduced last season, but apparently has had little or no effect on

Ryan's strikeout totals since he is the only modern pitcher ever to put together three consecutive seasons of 300 or more strikeouts.

Most consecutive seasons striking out 300 or more batters: 3, Nolan Ryan, California (AL), 1972–74 (Ties Amos W. Rusie, New York (NL), 1890–92)

Cardinal Lou Brock stole 118 bases in one season.

King of the Thieves

CHICAGO, Illinois, September 29, 1974—Lou Brock didn't let a threatening letter affect his on-the-field performance today as the fleet-footed Cardinal outfielder stole his 118th base of the season and rapped two hits in leading St. Louis to a 7–3 victory over the Chicago Cubs.

Brock, and teammate Bake McBride, had received death-threat letters in St. Louis 10 days ago, shortly after Brock had broken the major league record for stolen bases. It was in St. Louis against the Phillies that Brock stole a base for the 105th time this season, breaking Maury Wills' major league record of 104 bases swiped in 1962. Since that time, Brock, a .306 hitter, has stolen 13 more bases while the Cardinals were in the thick of a pennant race with Pittsburgh.

Most stolen bases, season: 118, Lou Brock, St. Louis (NL), 1974

Dodger reliefer Mike Marshall appeared in 106 games, including 13 in a row, in 1974.

Record Relief

HOUSTON, Texas, October 1, 1974—Relief pitcher Mike Marshall and his Los Angeles teammates prepared for the National League playoffs with an 8–5 victory over the Houston Astros in Harris County Domed Stadium here tonight.

Marshall, who earlier this year had appeared in a record 13 consecutive games as a pitcher, was not particularly effective as he gave up two hits, walked six batters, and yielded four runs in the two innings he worked.

But the appearance did nothing to dim the overall season's performance of Marshall, who is pursuing a doctoral degree in kinesiology at Michigan State in the off-season. He has appeared in

106 games, shattering his own major league record of 92 set last season with the Montreal Expos. Marshall's 208 innings were also a season's record for a relief pitcher.

Most games, pitcher, season: 106, Mike Marshall, Los Angeles (NL), 1974

Most innings pitched, relief pitcher, season: 208, Mike Marshall, Los Angeles (NL), 1974

Most consecutive games, pitcher: 13, Mike Marshall, Los Angeles (NL), 1974

PRO BASKETBALL

Boston's Bill Sharman made 93.2 percent of his free throw attempts in one season.

Dead-Eye Bill

BOSTON, Massachusetts, March 10, 1959—Boston's Bill Sharman quietly eased his way into the record book tonight in a game that saw the New York Knickerbockers defeat the Celtics, 138–116.

It was the regular season finale for both teams and Boston had already clinched first place in its division of the NBA. Richie Guerin and Kenny Sears each scored 22 points for the victors, while Bob Cousy collected 37, ten more than teammate Sharman for the Celtics.

But it was Sharman who made a contribution of greater significance. Although he hit on only one of eight field goal attempts in the first half, Bill was hitting from the free throw line with his usual deadliness. The Southern Californian made good on all seven foul shots as he raised his season's shooting percentage to 93.2 percent from the charity stripe, making 342 out of 367 attempts. The 93.2 percent accuracy is an NBA record.

Highest shooting percentage, free throws, season: 93.2 percent (342 of 367), Bill Sharman, Boston Celtics, 1958–59

Carom King

PHILADELPHIA, Pennsylvania, November 24, 1960—Disappointing a Thanksgiving Day capacity crowd of 11,003 at Convention Hall, the Boston Celtics strengthened their hold on first place by beating the Philadelphia Warriors, 132–129. But you certainly can't fault the Warriors' big Wilt Chamberlain, who hauled down a record 55 rebounds and scored 34 points, despite being guarded by defensive ace Bill Russell. Chamberlain's efforts off the backboards surpassed Russell's NBA record of 51 rebounds grabbed in a game against Syracuse last season.

Most rebounds, game: 55, Wilt Chamberlain, Philadelphia Warriors, vs. Boston Celtics, November 24, 1960

All-Star Boardman

ST. LOUIS, Missouri, January 16, 1962—Playing before the hometown fans, Bob Pettit of the St. Louis Hawks pulled down a

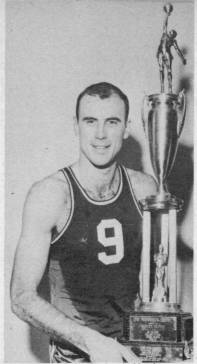

Bob Pettit of the St. Louis Hawks was a four-time MVP.

record 27 rebounds and scored 25 points as he led the West to a 150–130 victory tonight in the NBA All-Star Game. Pettit was chosen Most Valuable Player in this annual game for the fourth time, getting the nod over Wilt Chamberlain, who scored a record 42 points in a losing cause for the East.

Pettit had held both the former rebound record of 26 and the old scoring record of 29 points. The 6-foot 9-inch Hawk forward out of Louisiana State had good support in the West triumph as the Lakers' Elgin Baylor scored 32 points and Jerry West contributed 18. Cincinnati's Oscar Robertson added 26 points for the winners, while Chicago rookie Walt Bellamy scored 23.

Most rebounds, NBA All-Star Game: 27, Bob Pettit, St. Louis Hawks, January 16, 1962

Most points, NBA All-Star Game: 42, Wilt Chamberlain, Philadelphia Warriors, January 16, 1962

Wilt Chamberlain holds the single-game record of 100 points, set against the New York Knickerbockers.

Turn of the Century

HERSHEY, Pennsylvania, March 2, 1962—The Big Dipper shone tonight as Wilt Chamberlain rewrote the record book by scoring

100 points against the New York Knickerbockers in a regular season National Basketball Association game played here as one of Philadelphia's "home" games.

The 7-foot-plus Chamberlain, who attended Overbrook High School in Philadelphia before going to the University of Kansas, established single game records for most points, most field goals, most free throws made, and most shots. Along the way, he also set marks for most points in one half and most points and most shots in one quarter.

Chamberlain, a 61 percent free-throw shooter for the season, made his first ten shots from the charity stripe and converted on 28 of 32 overall to go with his 36-for-63 shooting from the field despite the defensive efforts of Knick center Darrell Imhoff, forwards Cleveland Buckner and Willie Naulls, and just about everybody else on the hapless Knick team, which lost, 169–147.

Opening up with 23 points in the first quarter, Chamberlain had 41 at the half and 69 before the third period ended. In the fourth quarter his teammates began feeding him consistently in an effort to break his own record of 78 points scored earlier this season. The final two points came on a dunk shot off a looping pass from Joe Ruklick with 46 seconds remaining in the game.

Most points, game: 100, Wilt Chamberlain, Philadelphia Warriors, vs. New York Knickerbockers, March 2, 1962

Most field goals attempted, game: 63, Wilt Chamberlain, Philadelphia Warriors, vs. New York Knickerbockers, March 2, 1962

Most field goals made, game: 36, Wilt Chamberlain, Philadelphia Warriors, vs. New York Knickerbockers, March 2, 1962

Most free throws made, game: 28, Wilt Chamberlain, Philadelphia Warriors, vs. New York Knickerbockers, March 2, 1962

Most points, half: 59, Wilt Chamberlain, Philadelphia Warriors, vs. New York Knickerbockers, March 2, 1962

Most field goals attempted, half: 37, Wilt Chamberlain, Philadelphia Warriors, vs. New York Knickerbockers, March 2, 1962

Most field goals made, half: 22, Wilt Chamberlain, Philadelphia Warriors, vs. New York Knickerbockers, March 2, 1962

Most points, quarter: 31, Wilt Chamberlain, Philadelphia Warriors, vs. New York Knickerbockers, March 2, 1962

Most field goals attempted, quarter: 21, Wilt Chamberlain, Philadelphia Warriors, vs. New York Knickerbockers, March 2, 1962

Most field goals made, quarter: 12, Wilt Chamberlain, Philadelphia Warriors, vs. New York Knickerbockers, March 2, 1962 (Ties Cliff Hagan, St. Louis Hawks, vs. New York Knickerbockers, February 4, 1958)

Making a Point

CHICAGO, Illinois, March 14, 1962—Wilt Chamberlain, who set a rebounding record last season, finished this year with a 34-point performance that gave him 4,029 points and a 50.4-point-per-game scoring average as he led the Philadelphia Warriors to a 119–115 decision over the expansion Chicago Packers.

The 7-foot Chamberlain, who created the NBA record of 2,149 rebounds during the 1960–61 campaign, was a scoring phenom this year as he set records for the most field goal attempts, most field goals made, most free throws attempted, in addition to his total points and scoring average. In one game this year, against the New York Knicks, he scored a record high 100 points.

Most points, season: 4,029, Wilt Chamberlain, Philadelphia Warriors, 1961–62

Highest scoring average, season: 50.4, Wilt Chamberlain, Philadelphia Warriors, 1961–62

Most field goals attempted, season: 3,159, Wilt Chamberlain, Philadelphia Warriors, 1961–62

Most field goals made, season: 1,597, Wilt Chamberlain, Philadelphia Warriors, 1961–62

Most free throws attempted, season: 1,363, Wilt Chamberlain, Philadelphia Warriors, 1961–62

Most rebounds, season: 2,149, Wilt Chamberlain, Philadelphia Warriors, 1960–61

Elgin's Precision Performance

BOSTON, Massachusetts, April 14, 1962—Elgin Baylor pumped in a record 61 points to put the Lakers one game up in the best-of-seven NBA championship series as Los Angeles beat defending champion Boston, 126–121. The Lakers lead the series, three games to two.

In upsetting the Celtics—who have won the last three league titles—Los Angeles came from behind to outscore Boston, 33–22, in the final quarter.

The 6-foot 5-inch Baylor, who played collegiate ball at Seattle, sank 22 of 40 field goal attempts and added 17 points at the free-throw line.

Most points, NBA championship series, game: 61, Elgin Baylor, Los Angeles Lakers, vs. Boston Celtics, April 14, 1962

Laker Elgin Baylor scored 61 points in an NBA championship-series game.

Boston's Bill Russell has twice pulled down 40 rebounds in a champion-ship-series game.

Bill on the Boards

BOSTON, Massachusetts, April 18, 1962—It took an extra period to do it, but the Boston Celtics won their fourth straight NBA championship today as Bill Russell hauled down a record-tying 40 rebounds in the 110–107 triumph over Los Angeles.

Elgin Baylor, who has been shuttling between the basketball court and Army duties at Fort Lewis, Washington, most of the season, led the losers with 41 points while Jerry West contributed 35.

But it was the heroics of Russell and Sam Jones that brought the Celtics an unprecedented fourth consecutive championship. After the Lakers' Frank Selvy had scored the last four points in regulation time to knot the score at 100, Russell and Jones took over in the overtime. Jones scored five points and Russell dominated the backboard while scoring four points as Boston outscored LA, 10–7, in the extra session. Russell paced Boston scorers with 30 points and Jones added 27.

Most rebounds, NBA championship series, game: 40, Bill Russell, Boston Celtics, vs. Los Angeles Lakers, April 18, 1962 (Ties his own record vs. St. Louis Hawks, March 29, 1960)

San Francisco's Guy Rodgers shares the NBA record with 28 assists in a game.

Helpful Guy

SAN FRANCISCO, California, March 14, 1965—Guy Rodgers passed his way into the NBA record book, but the playoff-bound San Francisco Warriors still lost to the St. Louis Hawks, 114–109, at the Cow Palace tonight.

The 6-foot Rodgers, who played college ball at Temple, contributed 28 assists, tying Bob Cousy's league mark. Despite the nifty passing of Rodgers, though, the Warriors couldn't overcome the 35-point, 13-rebound performance of Hawk forward Bob Pettit.

The main beneficiary of Rodgers' slick feeds was Wilt Chamberlain, who made 17 of 21 shots, most of them close to the basket following sharp passes from Rodgers.

Most assists, game: 28, Guy Rodgers, San Francisco Warriors, vs. St. Louis Hawks, March 14, 1965 (Ties Bob Cousy, Boston Celtics, vs. Minneapolis Lakers, February 27, 1959)

Cincinnati's Oscar Robertson averaged 11.5 assists a game in 1964-65.

O's Helping Hand

PHILADELPHIA, Pennsylvania, March 20, 1965—Oscar Robertson scored 20 points before he was injured and Jerry Lucas scored

34 points and grabbed 22 rebounds to lead Cincinnati to a 125–122 victory over the Philadelphia 76ers here today.

Robertson went crashing to the floor after being accidentally tripped early in the third quarter. The ankle injury kept the Big O on the bench for 18 minutes today and will keep him out of the season's finale, but the Royals already have second place clinched in the NBA's Eastern Division.

Before he left the game, Robertson chalked up nine assists, to raise his season's total to 861, an average of 11.5 per game. That's the highest assist average in NBA history.

Most assists per game, season: 11.5 (861 assists in 75 games), Oscar Robertson, Cincinnati Royals, 1964–65

Kerr-Age

BALTIMORE, Maryland, November 5, 1965—Baltimore coach Paul Seymour kept former teammate Johnny Kerr on the bench with a bad ankle tonight in Boston's 129–118 triumph over the Bullets and thus severed the longest consecutive-game playing streak in NBA history.

Seymour said matter-of-factly afterward, "Johnny had an injured ankle and we didn't want to take any chances."

The 6-foot 9-inch Kerr, a hook-shot artist out of Illinois, began his streak of 844 games on October 31, 1954, his first season in the pros. The big redhead was not a starter on the Syracuse team that included Dolph Schayes and Bill Gabor at forwards, 6-6 Earl Lloyd at center, and George King and Seymour at the guards. Syracuse lost that game, 97–94, to the defending champion Minneapolis Lakers, whose starting unit included Vern Mikkelsen, Jim Pollard, Whitey Skoog, and Slater Martin. Clyde Lovellette was at center in place of the recently retired George Mikan, who stepped down with the introduction of the 24-second shot clock at the beginning of the season.

In the 844th game of his streak, Kerr played last night in the Bullets' 108–107 loss to New York in Madison Square Garden. Kerr, who has played with only two teams in 11 years, Syracuse-Philadelphia and these Bullets, counts among his current teammates, Jim "Bad News" Barnes, Kevin Loughery, Don Ohl, Jerry Sloan, Johnny Green, and Bailey Howell.

Most consecutive games played: 844, John Kerr, Syracuse Nation-

Johnny Kerr (10) played with Syracuse, Philadelphia and Baltimore in
the course of his 844 consecutive-games streak.

Los Angeles' Jerry West lines up his 840th free throw, a single-season standard.

Sweet Charity

LOS ANGELES, California, March 20, 1966—Jerry West converted 11 of 12 free throws as he scored 35 points in leading Los Angeles to a 124–112 victory over the San Francisco Warriors here tonight. The loss prevented the Warriors from gaining a playoff berth in the NBA's Western Division.

The 6-foot 3-inch West, a six-year pro out of West Virginia University, created an NBA record with his free-throw shooting. The 11 tonight raised his total for the season to 840, breaking the old mark of 835 set by Wilt Chamberlain four seasons ago. West, who is called "Zeke from Cabin Creek" by his teammates, averaged 28.7 points a game this season.

Most free throws made, season: 840, Jerry West, Los Angeles, 1965–66

Deadly

SYRACUSE, New York, February 28, 1967—Wilt Chamberlain made his first four shots from the floor before he missed a whirling underhanded layup, ending a record 35-for-35 field goal shooting streak. Wilt went on to score 28 points tonight in leading the Philadelphia 76ers past Cincinnati, 127–107. The 76ers played in this upstate New York city for 14 seasons as the Syracuse Nationals before transferring to Philadelphia four years ago.

Chamberlain's shooting streak began 11 days ago against this same Cincinnati team in a 127–118 Philadelphia victory in Cleveland. The highlight of the streak, however, came a week ago when the Big Dipper dropped in 11 shots in 11 attempts in taking the 76ers to a 123–122 victory over St. Louis.

Most consecutive field goals: 35, Wilt Chamberlain, Philadelphia 76ers, February 17, 1967 to February 28, 1967

End of Laker Chain

MILWAUKEE, Wisconsin, January 9, 1972—The team defense of the Milwaukee Bucks and the individual brilliance of Kareem Abdul-Jabbar brought an end to the longest winning streak in

Milwaukee's Kareem Abdul-Jabbar lofts one over Wilt Chamberlain as the Bucks end the Lakers' 33-game winning streak.

major professional sports. Milwaukee defeated the Los Angeles Lakers, 120–104, before a sellout crowd of 10,746 and a national television audience this afternoon, ending the Lakers' 33-game winning streak.

The string of victories included at least one triumph over every other team in the league, including these same Bucks. The Lakers' effort, which began October 31, was the longest winning streak compiled by a major league team in basketball, football, baseball, or hockey.

The defeat came about because Milwaukee guards Lucius Allen, Oscar Robertson, Jon McGlocklin and Wali Jones kept rushing back on defense, cutting off the Lakers' fast break. Los Angeles had used the rebounding of Wilt Chamberlain and Happy Hairston and the quickness of Jerry West, Gail Goodrich, Jim Price, and Jim McMillian to run their way to victory in most of the 33 triumphs.

In addition to the defense by the Buck backcourt, Milwaukee center Kareem Abdul-Jabbar, the former Lew Alcindor, outplayed Chamberlain in the pivot and outfought Hairston under the boards as he scored 39 points and pulled 20 rebounds.

Most consecutive victories: 33, Los Angeles Lakers, October 31, 1971 to January 7, 1972

Tiny's Tops

KANSAS CITY, Missouri, March 21, 1973—The Kings' Nate "Tiny" Archibald, the only man ever to lead the NBA in scoring and assists in the same season, managed only six assists before being injured in tonight's game, but it was enough to give him a record 910 assists for the season. With Archibald sitting out most of the second half, Los Angeles beat Kansas City-Omaha, 124–118, in this final game of the season.

Archibald, who looks smaller than his listed height of 6-feet 1-inch and weight of 160 pounds, is a native of New York City who went to college at Texas-El Paso. He led the NBA in scoring this season with a 34.9-point-per-game average. His 910 assists, an average of 11.4 per game, broke the record of 908 assists by Chicago's Guy Rodgers in 1966–67.

Most assists, season: 910, Nate Archibald, Kansas City-Omaha Kings, 1972–73

The Kings' Nate Archibald set the season assist record and became the only man ever to lead the NBA in scoring and assists in the same year.

The Last Dip

OAKLAND, California, March 25, 1973—Wilt Chamberlain, who apparently can do anything he wants to with a basketball when he puts his mind to it, took his first shot at the basket in 75 minutes of playing time over a two-game span. It was his only shot of the night, and he missed it, but the Los Angeles Lakers still won this final game of the season from the Golden State Warriors, 96–89.

The Big Dipper, as Chamberlain likes to be called, was playing the final regular season game of his career, and scored one point on a free throw, pulled down 18 rebounds, and passed for nine assists. In his next-to-last game, against the Milwaukee Bucks, Chamberlain failed to take any shots at all from the field.

Throughout his career, the 7-foot-plus center has been something of a puzzle, although no one ever questioned his ability. In 1960–61, he set a mark for rebounding that still stands. The next year he broke virtually every shooting and scoring record in the book. In 1967-68, he led the league in assists, becoming the only man ever to lead the NBA in each of its three major statistical categories: scoring, rebounding, and assists.

After a 14-year career that included championships with Philadelphia in 1967 and Los Angeles in 1972, Chamberlain owns most of the career offensive records in the NBA, including the distinction of never having fouled out of a game.

Most points, career: 31,419, Wilt Chamberlain, Philadelphia Warriors, 1959-62; San Francisco Warriors, 1962-65; Philadelphia 76ers, 1965-68; Los Angeles Lakers, 1968-73

Most field goals attempted, career: 23,497, Wilt Chamberlain, Philadelphia Warriors, 1959-62; San Francisco Warriors, 1962-65; Philadelphia 76ers, 1965-68; Los Angeles Lakers, 1968-73

Most field goals made, career: 12,681, Wilt Chamberlain, Philadelphia Warriors, 1959-62; San Francisco Warriors, 1962-65; Philadelphia 76ers, 1965-68, Los Angeles Lakers, 1968-73

Most free throws attempted, career: 11,862, Wilt Chamberlain, Philadelphia Warriors, 1959-62; San Francisco Warriors, 1962-65; Philadelphia 76ers, 1965-68; Los Angeles Lakers, 1968-73

Most rebounds, career: 23,924, Wilt Chamberlain, Philadelphia Warriors, 1959-62; San Francisco Warriors, 1962-65; Philadelphia 76ers, 1965-68; Los Angeles Lakers, 1968-73

Most minutes played, career: 47,859, Wilt Chamberlain, Philadelphia Warriors, 1959-62; San Francisco Warriors, 1962-65; Philadelphia 76ers, 1965-68; Los Angeles Lakers, 1968-73

Nobody's name appears in the basketball record book as often as Wilt Chamberlain's.

Grit and Greer

PHILADELPHIA, Pennsylvania, March 7, 1973—"Greer," coach Kevin Loughery yelled from the end of the Philadelphia 76er bench.

At the other end, Hal Greer sat with his arms folded, watching his team taking its lumps from the New York Knickerbockers. The score was 73 for the Knicks, 57 for his team.

A ballboy sitting next to Greer nudged him and told him the coach was calling. The 36-year-old Greer jumped up and began peeling off his warmup suit. A murmur rose from the crowd of 7,069 in the Spectrum. Loughery gave Greer a few instructions, patted him on the backside and sent him into the game.

The murmur grew into scattered applause as Greer reported to the scorer's table. By the time he walked onto the court, the applause was deafening, it became a standing ovation.

The Philadelphia fans, suffering through their worst season ever, were paying tribute to the man who had played in more NBA games than anyone else: 1,122. The first game was back in 1958 when the franchise was in Syracuse and Greer was a rookie out of Marshall in his hometown of Huntington, West Virginia. The 6-foot-1 Greer played in 68 games that season and averaged 11.1 points a game. Every season after that he played in at least 70 games and scored in double figures. Along the way, he won MVP honors in the All-Star Game and played on the championship team here in 1967.

This year was different, though. Under a new coach, Roy Rubin, he played 37 games, but under Loughery, who replaced Rubin at midseason, the grizzled Greer was on the bench for 20 straight games. Tonight was the first time Loughery had sent him into a game.

Greer responded, hitting the one shot he took, grabbing a rebound and making four assists, the most of any 76er, although he played only 17 minutes. Greer also committed two personal fouls, which raised his career total to 3,855, another NBA record.

Most games played, career: 1,122, Hal Greer, Syracuse Nationals, 1958–59 to 1962–63; Philadelphia 76ers, 1963–64 to 1972–73

Most fouls committed, career: 3,855, Hal Greer, Syracuse Nationals, 1958–59 to 1962–63; Philadelphia 76ers, 1963–64 to 1972–73

Hal Greer played in 1,122 NBA games.

Oscar Performance

MILWAUKEE, Wisconsin, March 26, 1974—It was Oscar Robertson Night at the Milwaukee Arena and a full house was on hand to pay tribute to the greatest playmaker in NBA history.

Robertson, troubled by nagging injuries much of the season, made four field goals, converted six of six from the free-throw line, and made nine assists as the Milwaukee Bucks routed Kansas City-Omaha, 118-98. The six free throws gave Robertson 7,694 for his career, while the assists raised his pro total to 9,887, both NBA records.

The 6-foot 5-inch Robertson, who never played on a national championship team in college nor on an NBA champion until he came to Milwaukee four years ago, finished his career with 26,710 points, second on the all-time list behind Wilt Chamberlain.

Most assists, career: 9,887, Oscar Robertson, Cincinnati Royals, 1960–70, Milwaukee Bucks, 1970–74

Most free throws made, career: 7,694, Oscar Robertson, Cincinnati Royals, 1960–70; Milwaukee Bucks, 1970–74

West Is Best

INGLEWOOD, California, April 2, 1974—It wasn't much of a performance, not by Jerry West's standards, anyhow. But the veteran Los Angeles Laker guard had come off the bench tonight to play for 14 minutes and inspire his teammates to better efforts, bringing the Lakers their first victory in three playoff games with the Milwaukee Bucks, winning 98–96 before a capacity crowd of 17,505 in the Forum.

Elmore Smith was the real star of the game, scoring 30 points and pulling down 17 rebounds in outplaying Milwaukee's Kareem Abdul-Jabbar, who finished with 29 points and 15 rebounds.

But it was West—the all-time leading scorer in NBA playoff history—who provided the lift the Lakers needed. Sidelined since February 5 with a pulled abdominal muscle, West entered the game in the second quarter to a standing ovation. This—plus West hitting on his first jump shot—provided the spark. Jerry's totals

Oscar Robertson's helping hand accounted for 9,887 assists.

Los Angeles' Jerry West scored the most NBA playoff points.

were four points, two rebounds and an assist. And when he left the game, he was in pain again and wasn't sure he'd ever play in another one as a Laker. But he left behind his contributions, some of which are written in the record book.

NBA Playoffs:
Most points, career: 4,457, Jerry West, Los Angeles Lakers, 1961–70, 1972–74
Most field goals attempted, career: 3,460, Jerry West, Los Angeles Lakers, 1961–70, 1972–74
Most field goals made, career: 1,622, Jerry West, Los Angeles Lakers, 1961–70, 1972–74
Most free throws made, career: 1,213, Jerry West, Los Angeles Lakers, 1961–70, 1972–74
Most assists, career: 970, Jerry West, Los Angeles Lakers, 1961–70, 1972–74

Buckets by the Bushel

SAN DIEGO, California, February 14, 1975—It wasn't exactly a St. Valentine's Day massacre, but there was shooting aplenty to-

The New York Nets' Dr. J hit for 63 points in the longest game against victorious Conquistadors.

night as the San Diego Conquistadors and the New York Nets took four overtimes to decide a winner. San Diego finally took the American Basketball Association contest, 176–166.

Along the way, the two teams scored more points than any other opponents in pro basketball history, played the longest game in ABA annals (one NBA game lasted six overtimes in 1951 before the advent of the 24-second clock) and established countless league and club records. Almost lost in the welter of figures was a 63-point scoring performance by the Nets' Dr. J., Julius Erving, a personal high for him and one of the top 20 highest-point totals in all of pro history.

The Conquistadors, or Q's, as they are usually called, played like anything but the last-place team they are by getting clutch shooting from Travis Grant, Bo Lamar and Warren Jabali as they came from behind and prolonged the game. In the extra periods the Nets, defending league champion and currently on top of the Eastern Division standings, used outside accuracy by Billy Melchionni and Brian Taylor to keep alive.

The game took three hours and ten minutes to complete before a crowd of 2,916. Not everyone stayed until the end.

Most points scored, both teams, one game: 342, San Diego Conquistadors (176) vs. New York Nets (166), February 14, 1975

HOCKEY

Former Canadien Joe Malone scored seven goals for the Quebec Bulldogs against the Toronto St. Pats.

Goal-Getter

QUEBEC CITY, Quebec, January 31, 1920—Joe Malone, who led the National Hockey League in scoring in its first season a couple of years ago with 44 goals in 20 games, has another line in the record book. The new Quebec Bulldog, who came from the Montreal Canadiens at the beginning of the season, scored seven goals against the Toronto St. Patricks, more goals than anyone has ever scored in a single NHL game. The Bulldogs beat Toronto, 10–6.

Most goals, game: 7, Joe Malone, Quebec Bulldogs, vs. Toronto St. Patricks, January 31, 1920

Canadian Goose Eggs

MONTREAL, Quebec, March 14, 1929—Montreal Canadien goalie George Hainsworth recorded his twenty-second shutout in 44 games as he held the Maroons scoreless in tonight's season closer. Howie Morenz scored the only goal as the Canadiens beat their intra-city rivals, 1–0.

Hainsworth's phenomenal goaltending—he allowed only 43 goals all season—is all the more surprising in view of a rule change implemented by the NHL this season that was supposed to introduce more offense into the game. The change allowed forward passing in all three zones, a team's defensive zone, the center zone between the blue lines* and in the attacking zone. Previously, no forward passing was allowed in the attacking zone.

Most shutouts, season: 22, George Hainsworth, Montreal Canadiens, 1928–29
*Editor's Note: The red line at center ice was not introduced until 1943.

Ice Rocket

MONTREAL, Quebec, December 28, 1944—Before a holiday week sellout crowd of 12,744, Maurice "Rocket" Richard collected five goals and three assists tonight in powering the Montreal Canadiens to a 9–1 rout of the Detroit Red Wings.

Maurice "Rocket" Richard of the Montreal Canadiens totaled eight points in one game.

Richard's 8-point total—scored against rookie goaltender Harry Lumley—is one point better than the record set by Detroit's Don Grosso on a goal and six assists last February. The Canadiens' line of Richard, Toe Blake, and Elmer Lach scored a total of 16 points in the game.

Most points, game: 8, Maurice "Rocket" Richard, Montreal Canadiens, vs. Detroit Red Wings, December 28, 1944 (five goals, three assists)

Puck Feeder

CHICAGO, Illinois, March 16, 1947—Billy Taylor, having his greatest season after coming to the Red Wings from Toronto, fashioned a record seven assists tonight in sparking Detroit to a 10–6 romp over the Chicago Black Hawks.

Taylor assisted on three of Roy Conacher's four goals, as the Red Wings jumped off to a 4–1 lead before 17,071 fans in Chicago Stadium. The crowd enabled Chicago to establish an NHL attendance record of 521,777 in 30 home games this season.

Most assists, game: 7, Billy Taylor, Detroit Red Wings, vs. Chicago Black Hawks, March 16, 1947

Marathon Man

BOSTON, Massachusetts, March 22, 1964—The Boston Bruins were beaten, 4–3, by the Chicago Black Hawks tonight to finish last in the NHL for the fourth consecutive year. About the only thing for the 13,909 Bruin fans who jammed Boston Garden to cheer about was the performance of winger Andy Hebenton. The All-Star performer and winner of the Lady Byng Trophy for sportsmanship in 1957, Hebenton completed his ninth straight 70-game season. The first eight were in New York with the Rangers, and this season with the Bruins gave him a streak of playing in 630 consecutive games.

Most consecutive games played: 630, Andy Hebenton, New York Rangers, 1955–56 through 1962–63; Boston Bruins, 1963–64

Terrible Ted

DETROIT, Michigan, March 21, 1965—Inspired by the aggressive defense played by 39-year-old Ted Lindsay, the Detroit Red

In a career that spanned two decades, Ted Lindsay accumulated 1,808 penalty minutes.

Wings blasted the Chicago Black Hawks, 5–1, here today. Trying to top the NHL standings for the first time since 1957, Detroit got three goals from Gordie Howe in winning its thirteenth straight game on home ice before a crowd of 15,196.

But it was the play of Lindsay, who appeared in his first NHL game in 1944, that helped Red Wing goalie Roger Crozier hold Chicago to one goal. Along the way, Scarface, as the 5-foot 8-inch, 160-pound Lindsay is sometimes called, picked up three penalties to increase his career record total to 1,808 penalty minutes.

Most penalty minutes, career: 1,808, Ted Lindsay, Detroit Red Wings, 1944–57, Chicago Black Hawks, 1957–60; Detroit Red Wings, 1964–65

An official restrains Toronto's Jim Dorey (8), who racked up 48 minutes in penalties during game against Pittsburgh.

Battling Leaf

TORONTO, Ontario, October 16, 1968—Toronto rookie Jim Dorey collected a record 48 minutes in penalties in the first two periods before the game settled down and the Maple Leafs tied Pittsburgh, 2–2, on a pair of last-period goals.

After getting two minor penalties in the first period—when Pittsburgh opened the scoring on Bill Dea's goal—Dorey was slapped with 44 minutes in penalties in the second session: two minors, two majors, two misconducts and a game misconduct, which means he left the ice for good with 12:38 left to play in the scoreless period.

Most penalty minutes, game: 48, Jim Dorey, Toronto Maple Leafs, vs. Pittsburgh Penguins, October 16, 1968

Puck Stopper

NEW YORK, February 1, 1970—Filling in for the injured Ed Giacomin, 40-year-old Terry Sawchuk was minding the nets for the New York Rangers tonight and he stopped 29 Pittsburgh shots to chalk up the 103rd shutout of his National Hockey League career, as New York won, 6–0.

It was a memorable night on the Madison Square Garden ice as the Rangers' Dave Balon scored three goals for the first hat trick of

Terry Sawchuk recorded his 103rd shutout playing with the New York Rangers.

his career and Billy Fairbairn recorded three assists to establish a club scoring mark of 42 points by a rookie.

But the hero of the night was Sawchuk, Rookie of the Year 21 seasons ago, the only man ever to shut out more than 100 opposing teams. He did it with Detroit, the team he broke in with in 1949, Boston, Toronto, Los Angeles and the Rangers. This was Sawchuk's first shutout since the 1967-68 season, when he was with the Kings.

Most shutouts, NHL career: 103, Terry Sawchuk, Detroit, Red Wings, 1949–55; Boston Bruins, 1955–57; Detroit Red Wings, 1957–64; Toronto Maple Leafs, 1964–67; Los Angeles Kings, 1967–68; Detroit Red Wings, 1968–69; New York Rangers, 1969–70

Tony Esposito set the modern mark of 15 shutouts in a season as a Black Hawk rookie.

Tony Awards

CHICAGO, Illinois, March 29, 1970—Squat, but mobile, Tony Esposito recorded the fifteenth shutout of this, his rookie season, as the Chicago Black Hawks beat the Toronto Maple Leafs tonight, 4–0. Three days ago Esposito broke Harry Lumley's 16-year-old modern record with his fourteenth shutout of the season.

The modern era for goaltenders dates from the 1943–44 season when the red line at center ice was introduced. This line had the effect of speeding up the game by adding more offense since it allowed a player to pass the puck out of his own defensive zone. Previously the player would have to carry the puck out of the zone himself.

Nearing the end of a spectacular season, Esposito—whose brother Phil is a leading scorer with the Boston Bruins—should win both the Calder Trophy as Rookie of the Year and the Vezina Trophy as the league's best goaltender.

Most shutouts, season (modern): 15, Tony Esposito, Chicago Black Hawks, 1969–70

Here's Howe

NEW YORK, April 4, 1971—Gordie Howe, playing his last NHL game, was shut out tonight, as were his Detroit Red Wing teammates, 6–0, by the New York Rangers. It was the eighth shutout of the season for Ranger goalie Ed Giacomin, who with alternate goaltender Gilles Villemure will share the Vezina Trophy, emblematic of the NHL's top goalkeeper.

For Howe, who managed just two shots on goal, it may not have been a dramatic valedictory, but his career achievements will take a long time surpassing. This was the 1,687th regular season game Howe has played in since breaking in as a teenager in 1946, with Detroit, the only NHL team he has played for. Howe's career totals of 786 goals, 1,023 assists, and 1,809 points are all record amounts.

Most games, career: 1,687, Gordie Howe, Detroit Red Wings, 1946–71
Most points, career: 1,809, Gordie Howe, Detroit Red Wings, 1946–71

Most goals, career: 786, Gordie Howe, Detroit Red Wings, 1946–71
Most assists, career: 1,023, Gordie Howe, Detroit, 1946–71

Detroit's Gordie Howe ended his NHL career with a blaze of records.

Boston's Phil Esposito and Bobby Orr complete record-smashing seasons against Montreal.

Ice Masters

BOSTON, Massachusetts, April 4, 1971—Scoring right up until the last period of the last game of the season, Boston Bruin center Phil Esposito and defenseman Bobby Orr established three NHL records between them today.

With three goals, the 6-foot 2-inch, 210-pound Esposito, a native of Sault Ste. Marie, Ontario, demolished the old single-season record of 58 goals set by Chicago winger Bobby Hull three seasons ago. Esposito and Hull were linemates in Chicago for three seasons before Phil was traded to Boston.

In addition to his three goals, Esposito was credited with an assist in the Bruins' 7-2 victory over Montreal to give him 76 for the season and 152 points overall. The point total breaks his own record of 126 set in 1967-68, his first season in Boston.

As for Orr, who has been changing everyone's concept of what a defenseman should be, he assisted on a pair of goals, giving him a record total of 102 for the season. He is the only player to record more than 100 assists in a single season.

Most points, season: 152, Phil Esposito, Boston Bruins, 1970-71
Most goals, season: 76, Phil Esposito, Boston Bruins, 1970-71
Most assists, season: 102, Bobby Orr, Boston Bruins, 1970-71

Flyers' Hammer

PHILADELPHIA, Pennsylvania, April 6, 1975—The Philadelphia Flyers' Hammer struck in an unusual manner tonight, scoring a goal and waiting until only eight minutes remained in the game before getting into a fight. The Hammer, as forward Dave Schultz is referred to by his Flyer teammates, scored a third-period goal—his ninth goal of the season—in helping Philadelphia to a 6-2 victory over Atlanta in the last game of the regular season.

Eight minutes after scoring, Schultz and Ed Kea of the Flames were engaging in fisticuffs and were sent to the penalty box with major and minor penalties, much to the delight of the 17,007 fans in the Spectrum, who have learned to love the Hammer's roughhouse tactics. The seven penalty minutes tonight gave Schultz a total of 472 for the season, far outdistancing the record 348 penalty minutes he accumulated last year in leading Philadelphia to the Stanley Cup championship.

In last year's playoffs, the 6-foot 1-inch, 190-pound native of Waldheim, Saskatchewan, established another mark by racking up 139 minutes in penalties. This broke the record of 80 minutes by Montreal's John Ferguson.

Most penalty minutes, season: 472, Dave Schultz, Philadelphia Flyers, 1974-75
Most penalty minutes, playoffs: 139, Dave Schultz, Philadelphia Flyers, 1974

Philadelphia's Dave Schultz and his big stick add up to record penalties.

COLLEGE FOOTBALL

Army's Glenn Davis (right) set several collegiate records playing next to Doc Blanchard (center) and coached by Red Blaik (left).

Mr. Inside and Mr. Outside

PHILADELPHIA, Pennsylvania, November 30, 1946—The greatest era in Army football came to an end today as Mr. Inside and Mr. Outside played in their last collegiate game together. And it was almost a disaster. The Cadets, undefeated in three years (one scoreless tie with Notre Dame to blemish the slate) were saved by the clock. Navy, loser of seven straight after an opening game victory, was in possession of the ball on the Army 3-yard line, trailing 21–18 when the final gun sounded.

The crowd of 100,000, including President Harry S. Truman, had watched the Cadets open up a 21-6 halftime lead with Mr. Inside, Doc Blanchard, scoring twice and Mr. Outside, Glenn Davis, picking up the other touchdown. The score by Davis, on a 13-yard run after a pitchout from Arnie Tucker, was the fifty-ninth of his varsity career, giving him 354 points, an NCAA record. Before the day was out, Davis gained his 2,957th yard rushing for a record average of 8.26 yards per carry.

But nobody was thinking much about records in the second half of the game as Reeves Baysinger, Bill Hawkins and Leon Bramlett sparked the Middies to what would have been the greatest upset in the Army-Navy series.

Highest rushing average, major college career (minimum 300 attempts): 8.26 yards per carry (358 rushes for 2,957 yards), Glenn Davis, Army, 1943–46

Most points, major college career: 354, Glenn Davis, Army, 1943–46

Most touchdowns, major college career: 59, Glenn Davis, Army, 1943–46

Huskie Hugh

SPOKANE, Washington, November 25, 1950—Over land and through the air, the Washington Huskies were unstoppable today as they walloped Washington State, 52–21.

Washington's Hugh McElhenny averaged 14.8 yards per carry against Washington State.

Powerful Hugh McElhenny scored five touchdowns—including one on an 84-yard sprint in the closing seconds—and amassed 296 yards rushing. In doing so, he surpassed the Pacific Coast Conference single-season rushing mark set in 1948 by California's Jackie Jensen. McElhenny totaled 1,107 yards, seven more than Jensen. The Huskie runner also set a national record today. His 296 yards on 20 carries gave him a record 14.8 yards-per-carry average, a record for a single game.

Washington quarterback Don Heinrich, who threw for two touchdowns, eclipsed Chuck Conerly's season standard for completion. The Mississippi thrower had 133 in 1947, while Heinrich finished this year with 134.

Highest rushing average, game (minimum 20 carries): 14.8 yards, Hugh McElhenny, Washington, vs. Washington State, November 25, 1950

Mississippi Showboat

STARKVILLE, Mississippi, December 1, 1951—Although he had scored only three touchdowns all season, Arnold "Showboat" Boykin lived up to his nickname today and scored an NCAA record seven touchdowns in Mississippi's 49–7 rout of Mississippi State.

Boykin, a fullback from Greenville, Mississippi, ran out of the middle spot in the Rebels' split "T" formation when quarterback Jimmy Lear wasn't calling pass plays. Boykin scored on runs of 14, 12, 17, 13, 85, 1, and 5 yards, while Lear kicked all the extra points.

In addition to the victory, the Rebels will take the "Golden Egg" back with them to Oxford for the fifth straight year. The mounted gold football is symbolic of victory in this 50-year-old intra-state battle.

Most touchdowns scored, major college game: 7, Arnold "Showboat" Boykin, Mississippi, vs. Mississippi State, December 1, 1951

Jim Brown's Greatest Act

SYRACUSE, New York, November 17, 1956—Archbold Stadium was sold out today as more than 40,000 people were on hand to see Jimmy Brown in his last regular-season game as a collegian. The

Syracuse's Jimmy Brown scored 43 points in a game against Colgate.

All-American running back, who was born on a Georgia sea island and grew up on New York's Long Island, didn't disappoint
Syracuse fans as he put on one of the greatest one-man show's in
major college history.

Brown broke loose for six touchdowns and kicked seven extra
points in scoring a total of 43 points in Syracuse's 61-7 romp over
Colgate. The soft-spoken Brown picked up 197 yards rushing in 22
carries and scored on runs of 15, 50, 8, and 19 yards as well as a
pair of plunges from inside the 1-yard line. In totally dominating
the game, the Orangemen picked up 511 yards rushing, never had
to punt and intercepted five Colgate passes.

*Most points, major college game: 43, Jimmy Brown, Syracuse, vs.
Colgate, November 17, 1956 (six touchdowns, seven PATs)*

Rhome Not Built in a Day

TULSA, Oklahoma, November 26, 1964—Tulsa quarterback
Jerry Rhome was in there throwing today, completing 18 of 29
passes for 234 yards and two touchdowns as he completed a record-breaking collegiate career while leading the Hurricanes past
Wichita, 21-7.

During the season, the Dallas native was successful on 224 of
326 passes, an average of 68.7 percent. In addition, Rhome threw
198 consecutive passes without an interception, another record.
That streak, which started October 17 against Louisville, ended
today, not by an interception but by the end of the season.

Among Rhome's achievements are the most touchdowns responsible for in a game, when he passed for seven and ran for two
against Louisville; most points responsible for, in that same game,
with nine touchdowns and a two-point conversion; and the highest percentage of passes completed in a college career, 448 out of
713, for 62.8 percent.

Even though Wichita didn't win today's game, the Shockers did
manage to halt Rhome 26 yards short of the career record for total
offense. And Howard Twilley, Rhome's favorite receiver and the
leading pass-catcher in the country—who grabbed 10 tosses for 139
yards today—came up two points shy of the national scoring
championship. Twilley, who usually kicks extra points, got one
record this season when he scored six two-point conversions on
pass receptions. This ties the mark for two-point conversions for a
season and establishes a seasonal mark for two-pointers on passes.

Jerry Rhome threw his way into the record book playing for Tulsa.

Most consecutive passes without an interception: 198, Jerry Rhome, Tulsa, October 17 to November 26, 1964

Highest passing percentage, career (minimum 500 attempts): 62.8 percent (448 of 713), Jerry Rhome, SMU, 1961; Tulsa, 1963–64

Most points responsible for, game: 56, Jerry Rhome, Tulsa, vs. Louisville, October 17, 1964 (seven touchdowns passed for, two touchdowns scored, one two-point conversion passed for)

Lowest percentage of passes intercepted, season (minimum 150 attempts): 1.2 percent (4 of 326), Jerry Rhome, Tulsa, 1964

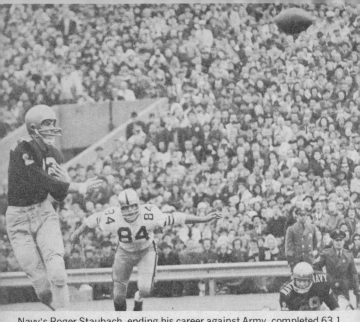

Navy's Roger Staubach, ending his career against Army, completed 63.1 percent of his passes during his varsity career.

Jolly Roger

PHILADELPHIA, Pennsylvania, November 28, 1964—Roger the Dodger Staubach did everything he could against Army today, but the Cadets hung in tenaciously to win, 11–8, and end Navy's five-year domination of this annual service school classic.

Staubach, the native of Cincinnati who scrambled his way to the Heisman Trophy as a junior last season, connected on 12 of 21 passes today for 110 yards. The figures raised his season totals to 292 completions in 463 attempts, setting an NCAA record of 63.1 percent for accuracy.

But in the end, it wasn't Staubach, but Army quarterback Rollie Stichweh who was the hero of the day as he engineered a 77-yard march late in the game that brought the ball to the Navy 3-yard line. That was close enough for sophomore Barry Nickerson to kick a field goal that made the difference.

Highest percentage of passes completed, career (minimum 300 attempts): 63.1 percent, Roger Staubach, Navy, 1962–64

Beware the Hurricane

TULSA, Oklahoma, November 25, 1965—Bill Anderson uncorked fourth-quarter scoring passes of 60, 63, 51, and 13 yards to give the Tulsa Hurricane a come-from-behind victory over Colorado State University today, 48–20. In addition, Howard Twilley caught two TD passes and kicked four extra points to give him 127 points as he became the first receiver ever to win a national scoring title.

Anderson, who had thrown only one varsity pass (incomplete) before this season while backing up Jerry Rhome, finished the year with a whole batch of records following today's 37 completions in 57 attempts for 502 yards and five touchdowns. Twilley, runner-up to Southern California's Mike Garrett in the Heisman

Tulsa's Bill Anderson holds more single-season passing records than any other collegian.

Trophy balloting this year, caught 19 passes for 214 yards today. The 19 receptions were one more than his previous single-game record.

Between them, Anderson and Twilley finished with these NCAA major college records:

Most passes attempted, season: 509, Bill Anderson, Tulsa, 1965

Most passes attempted per game, season: 50.9, Bill Anderson, Tulsa, 1965

Most passes completed, season: 296, Bill Anderson, Tulsa, 1965

Most passes completed per game, season: 29.6, Bill Anderson, Tulsa, 1965

Most yards passing, season: 3,464, Bill Anderson, Tulsa, 1965

Most yards passing, per game, season: 346.4, Bill Anderson, Tulsa, 1965

Most plays, season: 580, Bill Anderson, Tulsa, 1965

Most plays, per game, season: 58.0, Bill Anderson, Tulsa, 1965

Most yards gained, season: 3,343, Bill Anderson, Tulsa, 1965 (3,464 passing, minus 121 rushing)

Most passes caught, season: 134, Howard Twilley, Tulsa, 1965

Most passes caught, career: 261, Howard Twilley, Tulsa, 1963–65

Most passes caught per game, season: 13.4, Howard Twilley, Tulsa, 1965

Most passes caught per game, career: 10.0, Howard Twilley, Tulsa, 1963–65

Most yards gained, pass receptions, season: 1,779, Howard Twilley, Tulsa, 1965

Most yards gained, pass receptions, per game, season: 177.9, Howard Twilley, Tulsa, 1965

Highest average gain on pass receptions, career: 128.6 yards per game, Howard Twilley, Tulsa, 1963–65

Virgil's Standard

PROVO, Utah, November 5, 1966—Brigham Young's Virgil Carter thrilled a homecoming crowd of 30,184 today as his record-breaking passing performance carried the Cougars to a 53-33 triumph over Texas Western.

The slender senior, who is carrying a B-plus scholastic average while majoring in statistics, made good on 29 of 47 passing attempts for five touchdowns and 513 yards. In addition, Carter scrambled for 86 yards, giving him a combined total of 599 yards,

Brigham Young's Virgil Carter totaled 599 yards rushing and passing in one game.

an NCAA total offense record for one game.

While Carter, who received a standing ovation when he left the game with four minutes left to play, was working his aerial magic, his counterpart at Texas Western was gamely trying to keep the Miners in the game. Billy Stevens, one of the leading passers in the nation the last two seasons, completed 22 of 47 attempts but was hurt by three interceptions and a pair of fumbles.

Most total yardage, running and passing: 599 yards, Virgil Carter, Brigham Young, vs. Texas Western, November 5, 1966

77 Boots, All in a Row

TOLEDO, Ohio, October 4, 1969—Ken Crots was one of the few Rockets who misfired tonight as Toledo upset Ohio University, 34-9, in a Mid-American Conference football game in the Glass Bowl. It was the first loss for the Bobcats since 1967.

With a record crowd of 19,233 on hand, the Rockets rolled up their highest point total against Ohio since the series began in 1925. The point total could have been one higher, but for the fact that Crots missed a kick on the extra point following Toledo's second touchdown. This miss, the first of his varsity career, snapped his string of 77 consecutive points after touchdown, a major college record.

Fortunately for the Rockets, sophomore quarterback Chuck Ealey was on target and he directed Toledo to three more touchdowns, so Crots could start a new streak.

Most consecutive extra points: 77, Ken Crots, Toledo, 1967–69

Cardinal Performance

BERKELEY, California, November 21, 1970—All-American quarterback Jim Plunkett of Stanford completed 20 of 37 passes for 280 yards and a couple of touchdowns today en route to a collegiate record for total offense in a three-year varsity career.

Stanford's Jim Plunkett completed his regular-season career against California with 7,887 yards.

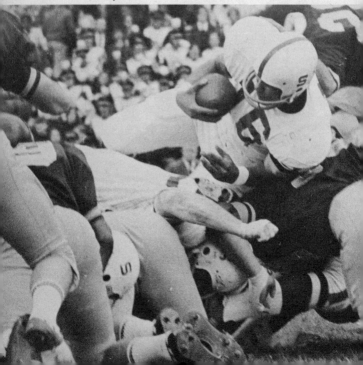

Plunkett also threw two interceptions and fumbled once as California handed Stanford its third straight defeat, 22–14.

The defeat was not very hard for Stanford to take, though, for in addition to Plunkett's record performance, the Stanford eleven was safe in the knowledge that they would be playing in the Rose Bowl January 1 by virtue of a stunning 24–14 victory over Southern California earlier this season. The Cardinals have an overall season's record of 8 victories and 3 losses.

In today's game, California had jumped off to a 13–0 lead when Plunkett hit little Randy Vataha on a 38-yard scoring pass. Then came a 74-yarder to Jackie Brown and Stanford had the lead, 14–13. California quarterback Dave Penhall rose to the occasion and directed a touchdown drive, carrying in from the 1-yard line himself, and the Golden Bears had their upset.

In his varsity career, Plunkett, a 6-foot 3-inch, 210-pound native of San Jose, completed 530 of 962 passes for 7,544 yards and 52 touchdowns. He also ran for 343 yards, giving him a record 7,887 yards in total offense.

Most yards gained, rushing and passing combined, major college career: 7,887, Jim Plunkett, Stanford, 1968–70

Flea Circus

LAFAYETTE, Indiana, October 30, 1971—Two running backs, each wearing uniform No. 24, were expected to provide the excitement today for the 66,339 fans who paid their way into Ross-Ade Stadium to see Michigan State do battle on the football field with Purdue.

The expectations were half-fulfilled, for Eric "The Flea" Allen, wearing Spartan green and white, scored four touchdowns and ran for a national record 350 yards as Michigan State routed the Boilermakers, 43–10. Otis Armstrong, who like Allen wears No. 24, but in the black and gold Purdue colors, was limited to 39 yards in 13 carries.

The 172-pound Allen, who played flanker last season, carried the ball 29 times and scored on runs of 23, 59, 30, and 25 yards. In addition, he caught two passes for 47 yards.

The record came on his last carry of the day, when the senior from Georgetown, South Carolina, sprinted around right end on a 25-yard scoring run. This gave him 350 yards rushing for the day,

Michigan State's Eric Allen rushed for 350 yards in one game.

surpassing by three yards Ron Johnson's performance for Michigan against Wisconsin three years ago.

Most yards gained rushing, game: 350, Eric Allen, Michigan State, vs. Purdue, October 30, 1971

Gator Aid

MIAMI, Florida, November 27, 1971—The Florida defense was lying down on the job tonight. In fact, the Gator defenders threw themselves on the ground in order not to interfere with Miami's John Hornibrook on his way to the end zone.

The unusual tactics were all part of a scheme to help Florida quarterback John Reaves capture a pair of NCAA passing records. There was only 1 minute, 10 seconds left to play and Reaves was still 13 yards short of the record set by Stanford's Jim Plunkett. But Miami had the ball. So the Gators, leading 45–8, let Hornibrook score in order to get the ball to Reaves once more. The 6-foot 4-inch native of Tampa didn't waste the chance, either, as he found Carlos Alvarez open 15 yards downfield and drilled the ball to him as the crowd of 37,710 in the Orange Bowl cheered wildly.

It wasn't just a one-shot night for Reaves, who completed 33 of 50 passes for 348 yards and four touchdowns in the 45–16 victory. In addition, Reaves caught a 17-yard scoring pass from halfback Tommy Durrance. When it was all over, Reaves owned the marks for most passes attempted in a college career, 1,128, and most yards gained passing, 7,549.

Most passes attempted, major college career: 1,128, John Reaves, Florida, 1969–71
Most yards gained passing, major college career: 7,549, John Reaves, Florida, 1969–71

Lions' Pride

KNOXVILLE, Tennessee, December 4, 1971—Penn State still has its Cotton Bowl bid and Lydell Mitchell has a couple of records—but Tennessee has the satisfaction of having beaten heretofore undefeated Penn State and holding the country's most prolific scoring team to 11 points.

The Nittany Lions, who will play Texas in Dallas New Year's Day, had their 15-game winning streak snapped as an alert Vol defense fashioned a 31-11 victory before 59,342 hometown fans.

Mitchell, a shifty runner teamed with powerful Franco Harris in the Penn State backfield, hauled in a John Hufnagel pass in the fourth quarter to score his twenty-ninth touchdown and 174th point of the season. Both are major college records.

But it was the play of Tennessee defenders like Bobby Majors and Jackie Walker that prevailed. Majors, younger brother of former Vol All-American Johnny Majors, ran back kicks for 195 yards, including one for a touchdown, while Walker scored on a 43-yard return of an intercepted pass. The victory put the Vols record at 9-2 on their way to the Liberty Bowl.

Most points, major college, season: 174, Lydell Mitchell, Penn State, 1971

Most touchdowns, major college, season: 29, Lydell Mitchell, Penn State, 1971

Pruitt Can Do It

STILLWATER, Oklahoma, December 4, 1971—Oklahoma's wishbone, which broke against Nebraska on Thanksgiving Day, was working like magic today as the booming Sooners rolled over Oklahoma State, 58-14.

With Jack Mildren pitching and Greg Pruitt catching, the wishbone "T" formation enabled Oklahoma to amass 584 yards on 69 rushing plays. Pruitt, who scored twice, picked up 189 yards and had sprints of 29, 32, and 64 yards. The junior from Houston, Texas, finished the season with 1,665 yards in 178 carries for an NCAA record average of 9.35 yards per attempt.

Mildren, the kind of running quarterback needed to make a wishbone attack effective, also scored two touchdowns in leading Oklahoma to its tenth victory in 11 games. The lone defeat came at the hands of top-ranked Nebraska on Thanksgiving.

Highest rushing average, season (minimum 150 attempts): 9.35 yards per carry (178 rushes for 1,665 yards), Greg Pruitt, Oklahoma, 1971

Oklahoma's Greg Pruitt has the highest single-season rushing average.

Mountaineer's Moment

MORGANTOWN, West Virginia, September 9, 1972—Mountaineer Stadium is nestled in the Monongahela Valley in the Appalachian Mountains, and the exploits of a West Virginia University football player today were nestled far down in the sports pages of America's newspapers. The big news of the day was the Soviet Union's stunning upset of the United States in Olympic basketball at Munich. Even Billie Jean King's successful defense of her U.S. Open title at Forest Hills rated more attention.

But W.V.U. junior Frank Nester—perhaps enjoying the lack of limelight—booted his way into the record book by kicking a record-tying six field goals against Villanova. The 170-pound American-style kicker attempted an NCAA-record seven field goals, and scored 19 points as the Mountaineers beat Villanova, 25-6. The lone Mountaineer touchdown came on a 20-yard sprint by Kerry Marbury in the second quarter.

Most field goals attempted, game: 7, Frank Nester, West Virginia, vs. Villanova, September 9, 1972

Most field goals, game: 6, Frank Nester, West Virginia, vs. Villanova, September 9, 1972 (Ties Charlie Gogolak, Princeton, vs. Rutgers, September 25, 1965)

'Husker Hustler

LINCOLN, Nebraska, November 18, 1972—Nebraska's Johnny Rodgers opened the scoring today with a 52-yard runback of a Kansas State punt for a touchdown and the Cornhuskers didn't stop scoring until they had whipped Kansas State, 59-7. The victory was the 100th in coach Bob Devaney's 11 years at Nebraska.

Rodgers also scored a touchdown in the second quarter, on an 8-yard run, before the game was turned over to the reserves. The touchdown on the punt return gave Rodgers a pair of NCAA records. It was the seventh time he had run back a punt for a TD, tying him with Oklahoma's Jack Mitchell in that department. Rodgers had also run back a kickoff for a touchdown, matching the eight TDs on kick returns by Colorado's Cliff Branch.

Most touchdowns on kick returns, career: 8, Johnny Rodgers, Ne-

In this game against Kansas State, Nebraska's John Rodgers tied two kick-return records.

braska, 1970–72 (seven punts, one kickoff) (Ties Cliff Branch, Colorado, 1970–71, [six punts, two kickoffs])
Most touchdowns on punt returns, major college career: 7, Johnny Rodgers, Nebraska, 1970–72 (Ties Jack Mitchell, Oklahoma, 1946–48)

Cardinal Cannonball

LOUISVILLE, Kentucky, November 25, 1972—Howard Stevens, the 5-foot 5-inch, 165-pound human cannonball in Louisville's backfield, scored two touchdowns today and established NCAA career records for most yards rushing and most points scored as the Cardinals beat Drake, 27–0, to tie the losers for the championship of the Missouri Valley Conference.

The victory was Louisville's second consecutive shutout and raised the Cardinals' record to 9–1 for the season. Strong as the defense was, however, it was the offense that made the headlines. Stevens, who started his college career at Randolph-Macon College in Ashland, Virginia, before transferring to Louisville, is credited with 58 touchdowns rushing, 69 TDs overall, both records, and 5,297 yards rushing, also a record.

Most touchdowns, career: 69, Howard Stevens, Randolph-Macon, 1968–69, and Louisville, 1971–72

Most touchdowns rushing, career: 58, Howard Stevens, Randolph-Macon, 1968–69 and Louisville, 1971–72

Most yards rushing, career: 5,297, Howard Stevens, Randolph-Macon, 1968–69 and Louisville, 1971–72

Big Boot

JONESBORO, Arkansas, November 23, 1974—Arkansas State's Joe Duren kicked three long-range field goals, including a record-breaking 63-yarder, to lead the Indians to a 22–20 victory over McNeese State.

Duren, a senior from Pine Bluff who uses the straight-ahead American style of kicking from placement, booted a 43-yard field goal in the first quarter and added a 56-yarder late in the game, in addition to his record-breaker. The previous longest field goal by a collegian was 62 yards by Mike Flater of Colorado Mines, last season.

The 63-yard boot, which had a little help from a gusting wind, equals the longest field goal kicked by a professional, Tom Dempsey of the New Orleans Saints, four years ago.

Longest field goal: 63 yards, Joe Duren, Arkansas State, vs. McNeese State, November 23, 1974

COLLEGE BASKETBALL

Seton Hall's Walter Dukes receives the MVP award for his play in the NIT.

Backboard Dukes

NEW YORK, March 14, 1953—No. 1-seeded Seton Hall had little trouble with St. John's University tonight as 7-foot Walter Dukes led the Pirates to a 58–46 victory and the National Invitation Tournament championship before a crowd of 18,496, the largest ever to watch a collegiate game in Madison Square Garden.

Dukes, the first Negro to win unanimous All-American honors, scored 21 points and pulled down 20 rebounds en route to winning the tournament MVP trophy. The 20 rebounds brought his total for the season to 734, an all-time record. Dukes is a native of Rochester, New York, where he was spotted working in his mother's dry cleaning store by Bob Davies of the Rochester Royals, a former Seton Hall star. Davies persuaded Dukes to attend Seton Hall, located in South Orange, New Jersey.

Tonight's championship was accomplished with the same ease that the Pirates displayed in compiling a 28–2 regular season record before sweeping Niagara, Manhattan and St. John's in the NIT. Little Richie Regan was the floor leader, racking up seven assists on feeds to Dukes and scoring 13 points.

Most rebounds, major college season: 734, Walter Dukes, Seton Hall, 1952–53

Furman's Frank Selvy scored 100 points in a collegiate game.

Have Gun, Will Shoot

GREENVILLE, South Carolina, February 13, 1954—Paladin
Frank Selvy used his gun often and well here tonight as he shot the

basketball through the hoop for 100 points in leading Furman to a 149-95 rout of little Newberry College.

The 6-foot 3-inch Selvy put on the show for his parents who were visiting with a few friends from his hometown of Corbin, Kentucky. The Furman senior, the leading scorer in the nation, started out with 24 points in the first quarter and added another 13 in the second. By the end of the third period, he had 62 and his teammates began to feed him the ball every time the Paladins were on offense.

By the middle of the fourth quarter he had broken the NCAA record of 73 points in one game, set by Temple's Bill Mlkvy in 1951. Selvy was also lucky that Newberry didn't try to stall or slow the game down in order to frustrate his shooting for the record. By the time the final gun sounded, Selvy had pumped in 38 points in the period to give him a nice round figure—100 points.

Most points, major college game: 100, Frank Selvy, Furman, vs. Newberry, February 13, 1954

Tar Heel String

KANSAS CITY, Missouri, March 23, 1957—For the second time in two nights, North Carolina was forced into triple overtime before emerging victorious as the Tar Heels defeated Kansas, 54-53, and won the NCAA basketball championship. The triumph was the thirty-second straight this season for North Carolina, a collegiate record for most victories in an undefeated season.

In the semifinal game last night, Lennie Rosenbluth hit two quick jump shots to lift the Tar Heels past Michigan State, 74-70, in a triple-overtime contest. And tonight, it was Joe Quigg's two free throws in the last six seconds of the third extra period that provided the one-point margin of victory. Even after Quigg had made good on the foul shots, he had to block a pass intended for Kansas' 7-foot center, Wilt Chamberlain, to preserve the victory.

Most victories, undefeated season: 32, North Carolina, 1956-57

Record Charity

DALLAS, Texas, March 6, 1962—Free throw shooting was featured here tonight as Southern Methodist used four foul shots in

Lennie Rosenbluth led North Carolina past Kansas with Wilt Chamberlain to 32 straight victories and the NCAA crown.

the last 61 seconds to defeat Arkansas, 84–81, and gain a tie with Texas Tech for the Southwest Conference basketball championship.

On Arkansas' side, Razorback Tommy Boyer made five free throws in five tries to cement his place atop the nation's free throw shooters. Over the course of the season, Boyer has made 125 of 134 free throw attempts for a record accuracy of 93.3 percent.

Highest free throw percentage, major college: .933, Tommy Boyer, Arkansas, 1961-62

Houston, which was led by Elvin Hayes (44) in its historic defeat of UCLA, posted a record 158 points a month later against Valparaiso.

Cougar Blitz

HOUSTON, Texas, February 24, 1968—With Elvin Hayes leading the way by scoring 62 points, Houston's basketball team scored an NCAA record 158 points in defeating Valparaiso, 158–81, here tonight. The No. 1-ranked Cougars—who ended UCLA's 47-game winning streak at the Astrodome last month—won their twenty-fifth game of the season and twenty-sixth game in a row.

In establishing a record for most points in a game, Houston shot 66 percent from the floor and outrebounded Valparaiso, 71–31.

Most points, one team, game: 158, Houston, vs. Valparaiso, February 24, 1968

Carr's Finer Points

DAYTON, Ohio, March 7, 1970—Hitting from long range as well as on driving layups, Austin Carr scored a record 61 points in leading Notre Dame to a 112–82 rout of Ohio University in the opening round of the NCAA Mideast Regional basketball tournament.

The 6-foot 3-inch Carr, a product of Mackin High School in Washington, D.C., broke the tournament record of 58 points set by Princeton's Bill Bradley in 1965. Carr hit on 25 of 44 field goal attempts and 11 of 14 foul shots for his 61 points.

Most points, NCAA tournament, game: 61, Austin Carr, Notre Dame, vs. Ohio University, March 7, 1970

Notre Dame's Austin Carr scored 61 points against Ohio U.

Prolific Pistol Pete Maravich of LSU ended his career in the NIT.

The Pistol's Parting Shots

NEW YORK, March 19, 1970—"Pistol Pete" Maravich, the highest scorer in major college history, was held to 20 points in the final game of his college career tonight as Marquette whipped

Louisiana State, 101–79 to advance to the finals of the National Invitation Tournament at Madison Square Garden.

Maravich was hampered by an ankle injury sustained in a quarterfinal-round victory over Oklahoma in which he pumped in 37 points. Tonight, not only did the Warriors double-team him, but they also choked off the passing lanes so Maravich could not feed his teammates with passes that are often as dazzling and unorthodox as his shots. The ankle injury will keep Pete out of tomorrow afternoon's consolation game against Jacksonville.

Maravich, who has played his entire varsity career under the coaching of his father, Press, thus finished with these collegiate records:

Most points, major college, season: 1,381, Pete Maravich, LSU, 1969–70

Highest scoring average, major college, season: 44.5 points per game, Pete Maravich, LSU, 1969–70

Most field goals attempted, major college, season: 1,168, Pete Maravich, LSU, 1969–70

Most field goals made, major college, season: 522, Pete Maravich, LSU, 1969–70

Most points, major college, career: 3,667, Pete Maravich, LSU, 1967–68 to 1969–70

Highest scoring average, major college, career: 44.2 points per game, Pete Maravich, LSU, 1967–68 to 1969–70

Most field goals made, major college, career: 1,387, Pete Maravich, LSU, 1967–68 to 1969–70

Titan Scorers

EDINBURG, Texas, March 6, 1972—Snubbed by the NCAA basketball tournament selection committee, Oral Roberts University tried to catch the eye of the NIT with a season-ending rout of Pan American here tonight, 108–91.

With 6-foot 3-inch junior Richie Fuqua leading the way, the Titans finished the year with the highest scoring average ever compiled by a major college team, 105.1 points a game. Fuqua, the nation's leading scorer with a 35.9-point-per-game average, pumped in 46 points tonight as Oral Roberts won its twenty-first consecutive game and twenty-fifth of 26 this season.

Highest team scoring average, major college season: 105.1 points per game, Oral Roberts, 1971–72

Notre Dame's Dwight Clay led the upset that ended UCLA's 88-game winning streak.

Bruin Power

SOUTH BEND, Indiana, January 19, 1974—A short jump shot by Dwight Clay with 29 seconds left to play provided a one-point victory for Notre Dame today, 71–70, as the Fighting Irish snapped UCLA's winning streak at 88, the longest in college basketball history. The Uclans had made Iowa their eighty-eighth consecutive victim in a game two nights ago at the Chicago Stadium, winning easily, 68–44.

The last time the Bruins had lost a game was on this same court three years ago—January 23, 1971—when Austin Carr's 46 points led Notre Dame to victory. Since that time, UCLA won its fifth, sixth, and seventh consecutive NCAA championships.

UCLA's record streak started January 30, 1971, with a 74–61 victory over the University of California at Santa Barbara. The Bruins depended on players like Curtis Rowe, Sidney Wicks, Steve Patterson, and Henry Bibby then. The next three years the mainstays were Bill Walton and Keith Wilkes. Today was the first time in their varsity careers that Walton and Wilkes were on the losing side.

The game between UCLA and Notre Dame was billed as a showdown between the teams' two centers, 6-foot 11-inch Walton and 6-foot 9-inch John Shumate of ND. Each scored 24 points, rebounded well and played tough defense. The difference was the ball-handling and shooting of Notre Dame's 6-foot 4-inch Gary Brokaw who scored 25 points, led a burst in the last three minutes in which the Irish outscored UCLA 12–0, and found Clay open for the final score of the game.

Most consecutive victories: 88, UCLA, January 30, 1971 to January 17, 1974

TRACK AND FIELD

Over the Hurdles

BATON ROUGE, Louisiana, April 2, 1960—It took a world record to do it as hurdler Don Styron led little Northeast Louisiana to a stunning defeat of defending Southeastern Conference track and field champion Louisiana State in a dual meet here today.

Styron won the 220-yard low hurdles in 21.9 seconds, clipping two-tenths of a second off the listed world record of 22.1, set by Gilbert Elias on May 17, 1958. In addition, Styron won the high hurdles and ran a leg on the winning 440-yard relay team. His brother Dave won both sprints and ran anchor legs on the victorious 440-yard and mile relay teams, while freshman John Pennel took the pole vault competition as the Indians from Monroe were winning 13 of the 16 events.

Besides the 220-yard hurdle mark, Don Styron is credited with a world record in the 200-meter hurdles, a distance about five feet shorter than 220 yards. The time of 21.9 seconds, same as the 220-yard mark, was made on a straightaway, with no turns.

World record, 220-yard hurdles, straight: 21.9, Don Styron, April 2, 1960

World record, 200-meter hurdles, straight: 21.9, Don Styron, April 2, 1960

Smith's Triple

SACRAMENTO, California, June 11, 1966—Speedster Tommie Smith of San Jose State added another world record to his credit as he sped 220 yards around a turn in 20 seconds flat tonight at an invitational track and field meet.

The 6-foot 3-inch junior from Lemoore, California, already owns the 220-yard and 200-meter records on a straightaway, both at 19.5 seconds, set just a month ago in San Jose. The 200 meters is about five feet shorter than 220 yards.

In clipping two-tenths of a second off Henry Carr's listed world mark tonight, Smith criticized his own performance. "It wasn't my best start, but I had a good lane, the third, and was able to keep my balance coming off the turn," he said afterward. "Sometimes when I come off the turn, the momentum throws me off. I know I can run faster."

San Jose State's Tommie Smith sets a pair of sprint records.

World record, 220 yards (turn): 20.0 seconds, Tommie Smith, June 11, 1966

World record, 220 yards (straight): 19.5 seconds, Tommie Smith, May 7, 1966

World record, 200 meters (straight): 19.5 seconds, Tommie Smith, May 7, 1966

Footballer O.J. Simpson ran on Southern California's world-record 440-yard relay team.

Trojan Horses

PROVO, Utah, June 17, 1967—Football players Earl McCulloch and O.J. Simpson joined with Fred Kuller and Lennox Miller on the University of Southern California sprint relay team in establishing a world record of 38.6 seconds today in the 440-yard relay. The time, set in the NCAA track and field championship meet in Brigham Young Stadium here, is four-tenths of a second faster than the pending world record set by this same foursome a week ago in San Diego.

McCulloch, who also won the NCAA 120-yard hurdle championship, got the quartet off quickly before handing off to Kuller. When Simpson passed the baton to Miller, a native of Jamaica, he was 15 yards ahead of his closest competitor, Tennessee's anchor man, Richmond Flowers.

World record, 4 x 110-yard relay: 38.6 seconds, University of Southern California (Earl McCulloch, Fred Kuller, O.J. Simpson, Lennox Miller), June 17, 1967

Bob Beamon shatters the world record in the long jump at the Olympics in Mexico City.

To the End of the Pit

MEXICO CITY, Mexico, October 18, 1968—Long jumper Bob Beamon was about to make his first jump of the Olympic Games. He pounded down the runway, hit the takeoff board in full stride and as soon as he lifted off the ground began flapping his arms as though he would gain greater height through flight. When Beamon landed at the far end of the pit here in Olympic Stadium, he was 29 feet, 2½ inches away from where he had started.

The 22-year-old Beamon, a native of Jamaica, Queens, in New York City, had broken the world record in the long jump by nearly two feet. The old mark of 27 feet, 4¾ inches was shared by Ralph Boston of the United States and Igor Ter-Ovanesyan of the Soviet Union.

World record, long jump: 29 feet, 2½ inches, Bob Beamon, October 18, 1968

Lee Evans posts a time of 43.8 for the 400-meter run at Mexico City.

Victory as Protest

MEXICO CITY, Mexico, October 18, 1968—Wearing black socks in silent protest over the treatment of other American black athletes, Lee Evans raced to a world record of 43.8 seconds in winning the 400-meter dash at the Olympic Games. Evans was followed across the finish line by Larry James and Ron Freeman, both American and both black, as the United States swept the event.

Evans wore the black socks to protest the dismissal of Tommie Smith and John Carlos from the U.S. squad after they gave a black-power salute on the victory stand following their first and third place finishes in the 200-meter dash. Evans' time of 43.8 seconds today was seven-tenths of a second better than the listed world record.

World record, 400 meters: 43.8, Lee Evans, October 18, 1968

Four for the Record

MEXICO CITY, Mexico, October 20, 1968—Lee Evans of San Jose, California, Larry James of White Plains, New York, and

Record-breaking U.S. 1600-meter relay team of Lee Evans, Ron Freeman (partially hidden), Larry James and Vince Matthews gives black-power salute on victors' stand.

Ron Freeman of Elizabeth, New Jersey, who finished one-two-three in the 400-meter run two days ago, were joined by Vince Matthews of Brooklyn, New York, today and the United States runners raced to a world record in winning the Olympic gold medal in the 1600-meter relay.

Matthews opened up with a 45-second leg, while the others with running starts were caught in splits of 43.2 seconds for Freeman, 43.8 seconds for James, and 44.1 seconds for Evans. Their time of 2 minutes, 56.1 seconds, bettered the old mark by 3.5 seconds.

World record, 4 x 400 meter relay: 2:56.1, United States national team (Vince Matthews, Ron Freeman, Larry James, and Lee Evans), October 20, 1968

Chi Cheng set the 220-yard record in the national AAU championships.

Chi Champ

LOS ANGELES, California, July 3, 1970—Chi Cheng, the 26-year-old California Poly at Pomona student from Taiwan, established a world record of 22.6 seconds in winning her trial heat in the women's national AAU championship track and field meet here today.

Just last month, at the Portland Rose Festival track meet, she ran 100 yards in the world record time of 10 seconds flat.

Chi, who competes for the Los Angeles Track Club, withdrew from the hurdle, long jump, and relay competitions in order to concentrate on the individual sprints.

World record, 220 yards, women: 22.6 seconds, Chi Cheng, July 3, 1970

World record, 100 yards, women: 10.0 seconds, Chi Cheng, June 13, 1970

Smith's Quarter

EUGENE, Oregon, June 26, 1971—UCLA junior John Smith beat out college teammate Wayne Collet en route to a world record time of 44.5 seconds in the 440-yard event at the Amateur Athletic

UCLA's John Smith breaks the tape in a 44.5-second quarter mile.

Union's national track and field championships at Heywood Stadium, here today.

Collet, running near the outside in lane seven, took the early lead and set the pace until Smith, in lane two, cranked up his sustained finishing drive and glided home two yards in front of Collet.

World record, 440 yards: 44.5 seconds, John Smith, June 26, 1971

Pan-Am Gold

CALI, Colombia, August 3, 1971—Jamaican Donald Quarrie easily outdistanced his rivals today in winning the Pan-American Games 200-meter championship and equaled the world record of 19.8 seconds. Marshall Dill of Detroit and Edwin Roberts of Trinidad-Tobago were deadheated for runner-up, a half-second behind Quarrie in the dash around one turn.

The 19.8-second time on the turn equals the record set by Tommie Smith in the 1968 Olympics at Mexico City. It was then that Smith created a furor by giving a black-power salute on the victory stand during the playing of "The Star Spangled Banner."

World record, 200 meters (turn): 19.8 seconds, Donald Quarrie, Jamaica, August 3, 1971 (Ties Tommie Smith, October 16, 1968)

Jamaica's Donald Quarrie establishes 200-meter record in the Pan-American Games at Cali, Colombia.

Kathy Hammond holds records in the 440 yard run and mile relay.

Stylish Runners

CHAMPAIGN, Illinois, August 12, 1972—With most of the male members of the U.S. Olympic team competing in Europe before heading for the Olympic games at Munich later this month, the U.S. women's track and field team stole the spotlight in setting a pair of world records here today.

Competing against the Canadian national team at the University of Illinois track, Kathy Hammond of Sacramento, California, created a world mark in the 440 with a time of 52.2 seconds. She then came back to lead the mile relay team to victory in the record time of 3 minutes, 33.9 seconds, shaving nearly five seconds off the old mark of 3 minutes, 38.7 seconds. The other members of the relay team were Mabel Ferguson, Madeline Manning Jackson, and Debra Edwards.

World record, 440 yards, women: 52.2, Kathy Hammond, August 12, 1972

World record, 4 x 440 yard relay: 3:33.9, Kathy Hammond, Mabel Ferguson, Madeline Manning Jackson, Debra Edwards, August 12, 1972

Man of Iron

SAN JOSE, California, May 5, 1973—It was Kentucky Derby Day today but Al Feuerbach—son of a veterinarian from Preston, Iowa—had his mind on things other than horse racing.

While the 3-year-old Secretariat was winning the spring classic in Louisville, the 25-year-old Feuerbach was breaking the world shotput record with a heave of 71 feet, 7 inches in an invitation track and field meet here.

The record came on Feuerbach's second throw of the day. He opened with a put of 70 feet, 10 inches, and then came the toss that broke Randy Matson's mark of 71 feet, 5½ inches set six years ago.

World record, shotput: 71 feet, 7 inches, Al Feuerbach, May 5, 1973

Steeplechaser

HELSINKI, Finland, June 27, 1973—For the third time this year, Kenya's Ben Jipcho has lowered the world record for the 3,000 meter steeplechase, with a time of 8 minutes, 14 seconds at the World Athletic Games in Olympic Stadium here this afternoon.

The grueling race over hurdles and through a water jump started out with Finland's Jouko Kuha—a former world record-holder in this event—taking the lead, much to the delight of the Wednesday afternoon crowd of 25,000. But halfway through the race, Jip-

Al Feuerbach throws a 16-pound ball 71 feet, 7 inches.

Kenyan Ben Jipcho holds trophy awarded him as the meet's outstanding athlete after he set the world steeplechase record.

cho took over the lead and gradually pulled away from Kuha and the rest of the field with the crowd cheering him on once they realized a record was in the making.

Only a week ago on this same track, Jipcho had run a 8:19.8 steeplechase, which broke his mark of 8:20.8 established earlier this year.

World record, steeplechase: 8:14.0, Ben Jipcho, Kenya, June 27, 1973

Stones High

MUNICH, West Germany, July 11, 1973—Dwight Stones returned to Olympic Stadium here, the same stadium where less than a year ago he won a bronze medal for a third-place finish in the Olympic Games' high jump competition.

Tonight, though, the 19-year-old native of Glendale, California, did a lot better than finish third. In a triangular track and field meet among West Germany, Switzerland, and the United States, Stones won the competition when he cleared 7 feet, 5½ inches. He had used a conventional straddle up to 6 feet, 10¼ inches before

Dwight Stones lands, then pleads for the bar to stay up at 7 feet, 6⅝ inches.

changing to the "Fosbury flop," the head-first backward-lunge style popularized by Dick Fosbury, Olympic gold medalist at Mexico City in 1968.

Even though he had already won the event, Stones had the crossbar raised to 7 feet, 6⅝ inches. He wanted to break the world record of 7 feet, 6¼ inches set by Pat Matzdorf two years ago.

Twice Stones tried and failed. Before the third jump, he took an extra long time to set himself mentally. Then he approached the bar in his usual wide arc, so that his back was toward the crossbar when he pushed off. Stones flung himself at the bar, going over head first, with his arms straight at his side. He brushed the bar ever so lightly.

The crowd of 25,000 hushed to silence as Stones stood in the pit, fists clenched, but silent, pleading with the crossbar not to come down.

When it stayed up, Stones leaped out of the pit and began a wild sprint around the stadium, to the amusement and applause of a crowd that had just seen a world record set.

World record, high jump: 7 feet, 6⅝ inches, Dwight Stones, July 11, 1973

Lightning Rod

SIENA, Italy, July 22, 1973—Rod Milburn, Opelousas, Louisiana's gift to track and field, continued his record-breaking ways in this history-rich and art-laden Tuscan town today as he equaled his world record time of 13.1 seconds in winning the 110-meter high hurdles at an international track and field meet.

The 23-year-old Milburn, a gold medal winner in the Munich Olympics a year ago, set the mark of 13.1 seconds in an invitational meet in Zurich, Switzerland, just two weeks ago.

Milburn, who attended Southern University, also holds the world record of 13.0 seconds in the 120-yard high hurdles.

World record, 110-meter hurdles: 13.1 seconds, Rod Milburn, July 22, 1973 (Ties his own record, set July 6, 1973)
World record, 120-yard hurdles: 13.0, Rod Milburn, July 25, 1971

Quick Rick

EUGENE, Oregon, June 8, 1974—Former Notre Dame star Rick Wohlhuter, now running for the University of Chicago Track Club, lowered his own world record in the half mile with a time of 1 minute, 44.1 seconds in the Heyward Field Restoration Track and Field meet here today.

Wohlhuter said he had come to the meet solely to improve on his time of 1:44.6 set last year in Los Angeles, and he did just that. Wohlhuter was not pushed to the record by a rabbit or close competition, and ran off by himself for most of the second lap.

World record, half mile: 1:44.1, Rick Wohlhuter, June 8, 1974

Joining the Ranks

LOS ANGELES, California, June 21, 1974—Steve Williams, a native of the Bronx, New York, attending San Diego State, equaled the world record in the 100-meter dash as he won the AAU national championship event with a time of 9.9 seconds.

Williams joins fellow Americans Eddie Hart, Rey Robinson,

Rick Wohlhuter breaks his own world record in the half mile.

Jim Hines, Ronnie Ray Smith, and Charlie Green as co-holders of the world record.

An English major at San Diego State, Williams had to hold off a strong challenge from Don Quarrie in the middle of the race. But at the finish line, Williams was far enough in front to be visibly pleased as he glanced back and saw his margin of victory.

World record, 100 meters: 9.9 seconds, Steve Williams, June 21, 1974 (Ties Jim Hines, June 20, 1968; Ronnie Ray Smith, June 20, 1968; Charlie Green, June 20, 1968; Eddie Hart, July 1, 1972; Rey Robinson, July 1, 1972)

Up and Over

GAINESVILLE, Florida, March 28, 1975—Dave Roberts needed three attempts to do it, but today he cleared a height of 18 feet, 6½ inches to establish a world pole vault record. Competing for the Florida Track Club in the Florida Relays, Roberts broke the record of 18 feet, 5¾ inches set by Bob Seagren on July 2, 1972 at Eugene, Oregon.

As a collegian at Rice Univesity, Roberts was the first man to win NCAA pole vault championships three years running, 1971-73. But the 6-foot, 2-inch, 185-pound native of Conroe, Texas, was performing inconsistently then, and he failed to make the U.S. Olympic team in 1972.

Roberts said he had been clearing 18 feet in practice and was confident he would eventually break the record. "But I wasn't sure it would happen here," he said afterward.

World record, pole vault: 18 feet, 6½ inches, Dave Roberts, March 28, 1975

Flying Saucer

LONG BEACH, California, May 4, 1975—San Jose policeman John Powell said he needed some practice when he came to the Long Beach Invitation track meet here today. "I came down with nothing in mind," the discus thrower recalled afterward. "I had no adrenalin flowing, I was treating this like a practice meet."

Dave Roberts makes his record-breaking vault in the Florida Relays.

The 6-foot 3-inch Powell "practiced" with a world-record toss of 226 feet, 8 inches. This discus heave betters the 224 feet, 8 inch effort of South Africa's John Van Reenen six weeks ago. And it betters the listed world record of 224 feet, 5 inches shared by American Jay Silvester and Sweden's Ricky Bruch.

World record, discus throw: 226 feet, 8 inches, John Powell, May 4, 1975

205

Man of the Century

WINTER PARK, Florida, May 9, 1975—Eighteen-year-old high school junior Houston McTear equaled the world record in the 100-yard dash with a 9.0-secone clocking in a preliminary heat of the Florida Class AA state high school track and field meet here today.

A native of Milligan who attends Baker High School in Okaloosa County in Florida's panhandle, McTear matched the time of Ivory Crockett set a year ago in Knoxville, Tennessee.

His time also establishes a national schoolboy record for the 100. He and Mike Roberson of Winter Park High School each had run 9.2-second dashes just last weekend in separate qualifying meets.

World record 100-yard dash: 9.0 seconds, Houston McTear, May 9, 1975

Bayi's Dream Mile

KINGSTON, Jamaica, May 17, 1975—It was billed as the "Dream Mile," and it came true tonight for Filbert Bayi of Tanzania.

Leading from wire to wire, Bayi shattered Jim Ryun's eight-year-old world record for the mile with a clocking of 3:51 in the Martin Luther King International Freedom Games. The 21-year-old Bayi, the first black to hold a world record for the mile, bested Ryun's record by one-tenth of a second and a formidable field including Marty Liquori of the United States, second with a 3:52.2.

It was Ryun who made his mark in 1967 as a Kansas University sophomore in the Amateur Athletic Union's national championships at Bakersfield, California. The mile standard had slipped downward from the time Roger Bannister of England broke the four-minute barrier with a 3:59.4 performance. Prior to that, the record had been lowered only 5.4 seconds in twenty years.

After breaking four minutes, Bannister observed: "There is no limit; man can go as fast as he wants."

World record, mile: 3:51, Filbert Bayi, May 17, 1975

Filbert Bayi of Tanzania holds the world record for the mile at 3:51.

GOLF

Walter Hagen won the most PGA championships.

The Streaking Haig

DALLAS, Texas, November 5, 1927—Walter Hagen rallied from three holes behind today to defeat Joe Turnesa, one up, and win his fourth consecutive Professional Golfers Association championship. It was the fifth time the dark-eyed, slick-haired Hagen, known as "The Haig," has won the event.

Turnesa did not give up easily, going one up in the first nine holes this morning, picking up another on the back nine and going three up on the first hole of the afternoon round. Hagen, a native of Rochester, New York, came on strong after that, however, and pecked away at the lead until he went one up on the thirteenth hole. The two men played even the rest of the way.

Hagen won his first PGA in 1921. Two years later he was beaten by Gene Sarazen in a memorable contest at the Pelham Country Club in New York. Since then, The Haig has won them all.

Most PGA championships: 5, Walter Hagen, 1921, 1924–27
Most consecutive PGA championships: 4, Walter Hagen, 1924–27

Link to Greatness

ARDMORE, Pennsylvania, September 27, 1930—The crowd around the eleventh green at the Merion Cricket Club hushed as Bobby Jones addressed the ball. Jones—trying to become the only man ever to complete a golfing "grand slam"—stood about 20 feet from the cup. He tapped the ball gently. It rolled toward the cup, but slowed too quickly. It did not have the legs.

The 28-year-old Southern gentleman from Atlanta was not really trying to make the putt, though. He wanted a good shot, but more importantly, he wanted to put the pressure on his championship round opponent, Gene Homans.

In May, Jones had won the British Amateur title at St. Andrews; in June he took the British Open at Hoylake and the U.S. Open at Interlachen, near Minneapolis. Today the U.S. Amateur was at stake. Jones had led all scorers in the 36-hole qualifying round of medal play and had breezed through the opening rounds of match play in the tourney. In today's 36-hole championship round, on the twenty-ninth hole, Jones was eight strokes ahead of Homans with eight holes left to play.

Bobby Jones completes golf's only grand slam in the U.S. Amateur championship at Ardmore, Pa.

The approach putt by Jones had set up a do-or-die situation for Homans. Both men reached the green in two strokes. Jones' putt was his third shot. Homans had to sink a difficult putt or lose, 8 and 7. Homans' shot never got close. Before the ball had stopped rolling, Gene was crossing the green to shake the hand of the only man ever to complete a golfing grand slam.

Most golf grand slams: 1, Robert Tyre Jones Jr., 1930

212

Queen of Swing

HOPKINS, Minnesota, August 31, 1935—The galleries were all rooting for 17-year-old local favorite Patty Berg, but Glenna Col-

Glenna Collett Vare won six national amateur championships.

lett Vare would not be denied today as she won her sixth women's national amateur golf championship on the Interlachen Country Club course here in this Minneapolis suburb.

Berg, a native of Minneapolis who started playing golf only four years ago, went down to defeat as Vare finished with two birdies to go up three holes with two left to play in the 36-hole final round of match play.

For Vare, it was the latest in a string of national titles that stretches back to 1922. She won again in 1925 and then three straight years, 1928 to 1930.

Most U.S. national amateur championships: 6, Glenna Collett Vare, Philadelphia, Pennsylvania, 1922, 1925, 1928–30, 1935.

Hogan's a Hero

OAKMONT, Pennsylvania, June 13, 1953—Ben Hogan shot a final round of 71 today to win the U.S. Open by six strokes and become the only American pro to win the event four times. The 40-

Ben Hogan shows the number of U.S. Opens he won.

year-old Texan benefited from a bad round of golf by Sammy Snead as the Slammer soared to a 76 and finished with a 289 for runner-up to Hogan's 283.

Hogan's four Open victories match the efforts of amateur Bobby Jones in 1923, 1926, 1929, and 1930, and Scottish-born professional Willie Anderson in 1901 and 1903–5.

In addition to Hogan's triumph at Oakmont today, he won the Open in 1948 at the Riviera Country Club in Santa Monica, California; in 1950 at Merion, Pennsylvania, and in 1951 at Oakland Hills in Birmingham, Michigan.

As for Snead, this is the fourth time he finished in the runner-up spot in one of the few major tournaments he has failed to win.

Most U.S. Open championships, men: 4, Ben Hogan, 1948, 1950–51, 1953 (Ties Bobby Jones, 1923, 1926, 1929–30; Willie Anderson, 1901, 1903–5)

Wright On

CHULA VISTA, California, July 12, 1964—Mickey Wright sank a seven-foot birdie putt on the sixteenth hole to take over the lead and hold on for a playoff victory in the United States women's open golf tournament here today.

Wright and Ruth Jessen were tied at 290 yesterday after 72 holes on the 6,400-yard San Diego Country Club course. Today's birdie putt on the sixteenth enabled Wright to finish with 70, two strokes better than Jessen in the 18-hole playoff.

The victory for the 29-year-old Wright—her fourth in the U.S. Open—brought her first-prize money of $2,200. Wright is the second woman to win four Opens, the first being Betsy Rawls in 1951, 1953, 1957, and 1960.

Most U.S. women's open golf championships: 4, Mickey Wright, 1958–59, 1961, 1964 (Ties Betsy Rawls, 1951, 1953, 1957, 1960)

Open Record

ROCHESTER, New York, June 16, 1968—In only his second year on the professional golf circuit, Lee Trevino fired a record-equaling 275 to win the U.S. Open championship on the 6,962-yard Oak Hill Country Club course.

Lee Trevino sinks a birdie which helped him to his record-tying 275 in the U.S. Open.

The 28-year-old Mexican-American who lives outside of El Paso, Texas, took the event by four strokes over defending champion Jack Nicklaus. It was Nicklaus who established the 275-stroke tournament record last year at Baltusrol in Springfield, New Jersey.

Trevino, an ex-Marine, played steady golf throughout the Open as he shot rounds of 69, 68, 69, and 69 on the par-70 course.

Lowest score, U.S. Open golf tournament: 275, Lee Trevino at the Oak Hill Country Club, Rochester, New York, 1968 (Ties Jack Nicklaus at Baltusrol, Springfield, New Jersey, 1967)

Five-Time Master

AUGUSTA, Georgia, April 13, 1975—A 40-foot birdie putt on the 16th green gave Jack Nicklaus the one-stroke margin he needed today to become the first five-time winner of the Masters golf tournament.

After 36 holes, Nicklaus held a comfortable five-stroke advantage, but then came charges by Tom Weiskopf and Johnny Miller that fell just short. As it was, Nicklaus had to sweat out a possible 18-hole playoff as both Miller and Weiskopf narrowly missed birdie putts on the 18th green only minutes after Nicklaus completed

Jack Nicklaus blasts out of the sand en route to his fifth Masters championship.

his four-under-par round of 68 to give him a tournament total of 276.

Nicklaus' triumph gave him sole possession of the record for most Masters victories, breaking a tie with Arnold Palmer at four. The Golden Bear, as Nicklaus is known, also won the green blazer emblematic of Masters supremacy in 1963, 1965, 1966 and 1972.

In addition to Nicklaus' record performance, several other marks were established. In the third round yesterday, Miller started the day by taking only thirty strokes to cover the front nine. In the process he shot a record 6 consecutive birdies on holes 2 through 7. Miller's final 36-hole total of 131 set another mark. And Hale Irwin turned the course upside down today with a record-tying 64.

But the day belonged to the 35-year-old Nicklaus, who saw his victory assured while standing in the scorer's tent.

The triumph raised his golf earnings to $2,392,865, which keeps Jack at the top of the all-time list in that category.

Most Masters Tournament victories: 5, Jack Nicklaus, 1963, 1965, 1966, 1972, 1975

TENNIS

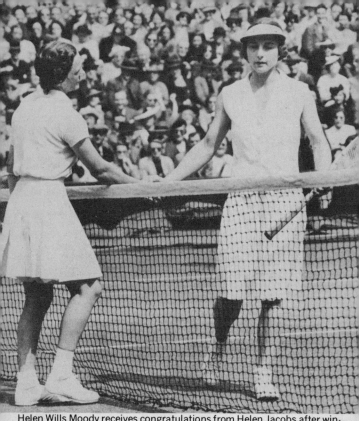

Helen Wills Moody receives congratulations from Helen Jacobs after winning her eighth Wimbledon singles title.

Moody Triumph

WIMBLEDON, England, June 2, 1938—Helen Wills Moody, who was among the first to shed the long-sleeve, ankle-length tennis dress, swept to her eighth singles title at the All-England tennis tournament here today by defeating Helen Hull Jacobs.

The victory, 6–4, 6–0, was assured after the eighth game of the first set when Jacobs reinjured her ankle and was virtually immobile on the court the rest of the match.

In a competition that was less than friendly between these two California residents, Jacobs asked no quarter and Moody gave none. This was the twelfth time these two women had met in a championship showdown.

Moody, who was known as "Little Miss Poker Face" in her younger days, won her first singles title at Wimbledon in 1927, the first of four straight. Her other championshps came in 1932, 1933, and 1935.

Most Wimbledon singles titles: 8, Helen Wills Moody, 1927–30, 1932–33, 1935, 1938

Rod's Slam

NEW YORK, September 8, 1969—Rod Laver beat fellow Australian Tony Roche, 7–9, 6–1, 6–2, 6–2, to win the U.S. Open championship at the West Side Tennis Club in Forest Hills today and became the first man ever to complete two tennis grand slams.

The lefthanded Laver duplicated his feat of 1962 when, as an amateur, he won the singles titles at the Australian, French, Wimbledon, and Forest Hills tournaments. This year the 31-year-old Aussie is a pro and earned $16,000 for the U.S. title alone.

The only other man to win a grand slam was American Don Budge, who achieved the honor as an amateur in 1938.

Most tennis grand slams: 2, Rod Laver, Australia, 1962, 1969

Australia's Rod Laver completes his second grand slam in the U.S. Open.

Margaret Smith Court defeats Rosemary Casals in the U.S. Open to match Maureen Connolly's grand slam.

Court's Court

NEW YORK, September 13, 1970—Australia's Margaret Smith Court defeated Rosemary Casals today to win the U.S. Open tennis championship at Forest Hills and became only the second woman to complete a tennis grand slam.

The 5-foot 9-inch, 145-pound Court came into the match after having defeated Kerry Melville for the Australian title, Helga Niessen for the French championship, and Billie Jean King for Wimbledon honors. All of those were in straight sets. On the center court of the West Side Tennis Club today, however, Casals pushed Court to three sets before the green-eyed Australian prevailed, 6–2, 2–6, 6–1.

Court's sweep of the four national championships duplicates the feat of American Maureen "Little Mo" Connolly in 1953.

Most tennis grand slams, women: 1, Margaret Smith Court, Australia, 1970 (Ties Maureen Connolly, 1953)

BOXING

Boxing's knockout king, Archie Moore, won the light heavyweight title from Joey Maxim in 1952.

Moore Knockouts

PHOENIX, Arizona, March 15, 1963—Former light heavyweight champion Archie Moore "unretired" tonight to pound professional wrestler Mike DiBiase for two rounds and 29 seconds before the fight was called, a technical knockout.

The 50-year-old Moore, who has been boxing for 28 years, had his first knockout in his first professional fight in Hot Springs,

Arkansas, against the Poco Kid. Moore has more knockouts to his credit than any other man who stepped into the ring, but exactly how many—like his date of birth—is a point of contention. *Ring Magazine Encyclopedia,* which does not differentiate between knockouts and technical knockouts, credits Moore with 140.

Accuracy with numbers has never bothered Moore, who won his light heavyweight title from Joey Maxim in 1952. He claims December 13, 1916, as his birthday, but his mother maintained Archibald Lee Wright was born in 1913 in Benoit, Mississippi.

Most knockouts, professional career: 140, Archie Moore, 1935–63

AUTO RACING

A.J. Foyt crosses the finish line for his third Indianapolis 500 victory.

A.J.'s Way

INDIANAPOLIS, Indiana, May 31, 1967—Anthony Joseph Foyt, Jr. of Houston, Texas, driving a car of his own design, won the rain-delayed Indianapolis 500 today and became the fourth man to win the classic auto race three times. A.J., as the 32-year-old Foyt is known, took the lead after Parnelli Jones' turbine-powered car was forced to drop out with only three laps remaining in the race. Jones had a 45-second lead over Foyt at the time.

Foyt, whose victories in 1961 and 1964 came in front-mounted Offenhauser-powered racers, drove the Sheraton-Thompson Special today. It had a Ford engine mounted on the rear of a Coyote chassis. In winning the 500, which had been set back a day because of rain, Foyt averaged 151.207 miles an hour. He joins Louis Meyer, Wilbur Shaw and Mauri Rose as triple winners.

Most victories, Indianapolis 500: 3, A.J. Foyt Jr., 1961, 1964, 1967 (Ties Louis Meyer, 1928, 1933, 1936; Wilbur Shaw, 1937, 1938–39; Mauri Rose, 1941, 1947–48)

Mark Donohue leads on the final lap of his record-setting performance at Indianapolis.

Mark's Mark

INDIANAPOLIS, Indiana, May 27, 1972—Mark Donohue, driving a McLaren-Offenhauser, took the lead with 13 laps to go and went on to win the Indianapolis 500 today by nearly a full lap with a record average speed of 163.465 miles per hour. Donohue finished ahead of Jerry Grant, one of Dan Gurney's All-American Racers, who was driving an Eagle-Offenhauser.

Bobby Unser, who had set a trial lap record of 196.678 miles per hour two weeks ago, was a big disappointment. Starting from the pole position, Unser was forced out of the race after 31 laps because of a broken distributor rotor.

As so often happens in the 500, the winner was blessed with a little luck. Donohue was cruising along in third position late in the race when leader Gary Bettenhausen was sidelined with an ignition malfunction. Then Grant, in second place ahead of Donohue, developed a flat tire and was forced into the pits. It was then that Donohue, who also set a single lap record by going 187.539 miles an hour on the 150th lap of the 200-lap race, took the lead and kept it to win his first 500.

Fastest average time, Indianapolis 500: 163.465 m.p.h., Mark Donohue, Newton Square, Pennsylvania, May 27, 1972

Fastest lap, Indianapolis 500: 187.539 m.p.h., Mark Donohue, Newton Square, Pennsylvania, May 27, 1972

Fastest trial lap, Indianapolis 500: 196.678 m.p.h., Bobby Unser, Albuquerque, New Mexico, May 14, 1972

SWIMMING

Mark Spitz butterflies his way to a seventh Olympic gold medal.

Spitz's Spritz

MUNICH, West Germany, September 4, 1972—Mark Spitz picked up his seventh Olympic gold medal tonight as he swam the butterfly leg of the winning United States 400-meter medley relay team. And for the seventh time in these Olympic Games, the 22-year-old Spitz was in on a world record.

A native of California who attended Indiana University, Spitz also set world marks in the individual 100- and 200-meter freestyle events, the 100- and 200-meter butterfly races, and in anchoring the winning 400-meter and 800-meter freestyle relay teams.

The 6-foot, 160-pound Spitz—whose extraordinarily long legs enable him to kick deeper in the water than most swimmers—is the first individual to win seven gold medals in a single Olympic Games. Three others had won as many as five, but no one had ever won more than that.

Most gold medals, one Olympics: 7, Mark Spitz, United States, 1972

HORSE RACING

Trainer Ben Jones, with his sixth Kentucky Derby winner, Hill Gail, Eddie Arcaro up.

Half-Dozen Roses

LOUISVILLE, Kentucky, May 3, 1952—"Plain Ben" Jones led a parade of familiar faces to the winner's circle today after 11–10 favorite Hill Gail won the seventy-eighth running of the Kentucky Derby. The race was televised coast-to-coast for the first time.

This was the sixth time Jones had tightened the girth on a Derby winner, a record number of victories among trainers. It was also the fifth time Eddie Arcaro had ridden the winner. And it was the fifth time a Calumet Farm horse had won. Mrs. Warren Wright, widow of the Calumet owner, accepted the trophy.

The race itself was not without its suspense, for Hill Gail—who broke from the inside post position—swerved to the outside shortly after the start. After about a half mile, though, Arcaro got a hold on the horse and kept him in front for the remainder of the mile and a quarter classic to finish two lengths in front of Sub Fleet, owned by Charles T. Fisher's Dixiana Farm.

Jones, the grand old man of Derby Racing, saddled Triple Crown winners Whirlaway in 1941 and Citation in 1948, as well as Lawrin in 1938, Pensive in 1944, and Ponder in 1949.

Most Kentucky Derby winners, trainer: 6, Ben Jones—1938, Lawrin; 1941, Whirlaway; 1944, Pensive; 1948, Citation; 1949, Ponder; and 1952, Hill Gail

Majestic Prince carries Bill Hartack to his fifth Kentucky Derby win.

Majestic Hartack

LOUISVILLE, Kentucky, May 3, 1969—Undefeated Majestic Prince out of California, Richard Nixon out of Washington, and Arts and Letters out of New York helped draw the first 100,000-

plus crowd into Churchill Downs for the Kentucky Derby today. And when it was all over, the President and 106,332 others had seen Frank McMahon's Majestic Prince engage Rokeby Farm's Arts and Letters at the quarter pole, and the two raced almost as one to the wire where Majestic Prince—ridden by Bill Hartack—earned the decision by a neck.

The victory for Hartack was his fifth in the Derby, matching the record number of triumphs by Eddie Arcaro. At the same time, trainer Johnny Longden, who crode Count Fleet to victory here in 1943, became the first man to have both ridden and saddled a Derby winner.

Most Kentucky Derby winners, jockey: 5, Bill Hartack—1957, Iron Leige; 1960, Venetian Way; 1962, Decidedly; 1964, Northern Dancer; and 1969, Majestic Prince (Ties Eddie Arcaro—1938, Lawrin; 1941, Whirlaway; 1945, Hoop Jr.; 1948, Citation; and 1952, Hill Gail)

Derby Double

LOUISVILLE, Kentucky, May 5, 1973—Canadian trainer Lucien Laurin put Canadian jockey Ron Turcotte aboard American-owned and bred Secretariat and the big chestnut colt ran himself into the Churchill Downs winner's circle and Turcotte into the Kentucky Derby record book.

Secretariat, owned by Meadow Stable, as was last year's Derby winner Riva Ridge, completed this ninety-ninth running in record time of 1 minute, 59 2/5 seconds in beating Sigmund Sommer's Sham by two and a half lengths.

Turcotte, who rode Riva Ridge in last year's Run for the Roses, became the fourth rider to bring home two horses first in consecutive Derbys. The others were black jockeys Isaac Murphy in 1890 and 1891, and Jimmy Winkfield, 1901 and 1902, and Bobby Ussery in 1967 and 1968, although Ussery's achievement is tainted by the fact that his 1968 winner, Dancer's Image, was eventually disqualified from first place after several years of legal and court battles.

Most consecutive Kentucky Derby winners, jockey: 2, Ron Turcotte—1972, Riva Ridge, and 1973, Secretariat (Ties Isaac Murphy—1890, Riley, and 1891, Kingman; Jimmy Winkfield—1901, His Eminence, and 1902, Alan-a-Dale; Bobby Ussery—1967, Proud Clarion, and 1968, Dancer's Image)

Ron Turcotte, aboard Secretariat, becomes the fourth jockey to run consecutive Kentucky Derby winners.

Record Ride

LAUREL, Maryland, December 31, 1974—One year ago today, an 18-year-old boy was in the stands at Laurel Race Course here and watched Sandy Hawley ride a horse to victory for the 515th time in the year 1973. Never in thoroughbred history had any jockey been aboard more than 500 winners in a calendar year, and Hawley established a record that many observers felt would stand for years to come.

One of those who agreed was the 18-year-old Chris McCarron, who was willing to "bet anything that Sandy's record will stand for 20 years." McCarron was a qualified observer since his older brother Gregg was a jockey, and he himself worked as a stable hand at the racetrack.

A month after Hawley's ride, McCarron received his jockey's license and rode his first horse, late in January. On February 9 of this year, young Chris rode the first winner of his life. By December 17, just two weeks ago, McCarron showed what he was made

Chris McCarron, 18, brought 546 horses home first in 1974.

of as he rode Ohmylove to a neck victory, beating a horse ridden by brother Gregg. The trip to the winner's circle was the 516th for young McCarron, breaking the not-quite-year-old record established by Hawley.

Chris is an apprentice rider, receiving an advantage in the weight his horses must carry because of his inexperience. But what he lacks in experience, he makes up in ability. Once he realized the record was within his reach, he began riding seven days a week. He rode here in Maryland Monday through Saturday, and on Sundays traveled to the Penn National course near Harrisburg, Pennsylvania. He became only the second rider to surpass the 500 victory mark in one year. Then he broke the all-time record. And in today's seventh race, on the last day of the year, he rode Sarah Percy to victory in the feature race of the day. The mare was a 3–5 favorite, and McCarron made the chalk players happy by bringing her home three and a half lengths in front for his 546th victory of the year.

Most winners, year, jockey: 546, Chris McCarron, 1974

Purse Snatcher

ARCADIA, California, December 31, 1974—New Year's Eve celebrations were already underway in some parts of the country

Horses ridden by Laffit Pincay Jr. won $4,231,441 in purses in 1974.

when Laffit Pincay Jr. got the leg up on Jestacepter for the ninth race at Santa Anita Park here.

Pincay, a native of Panama, had established an all-time record last year by riding horses who won $4,251,060 in purse money. He was the first jockey to go over the $4-million mark in a single calendar year.

And this year, the 28-year-old Pincay surpassed his previous efforts. By December 13, he had broken his former mark. But since that time, he had received a challenge from Angel Cordero Jr. for the jockey winning the most money. As of three days ago, last Saturday, both he and Cordero had ridden the winners of more than $4.2 million, Cordero at Aqueduct in New York and Pincay here in California. But Cordero was suspended seven days for a riding infraction and would have to miss the last two days of the year. Pincay didn't have to worry very much about retaining his title and establishing another record.

On today's card, however, Pincay failed to be aboard a winner for the first eight races. In the ninth, though, he brought Jestacepter home first in a race where the winner's share of the purse was $4,400. This boosted Pincay's total to $4,231,441. And since the jockey usually receives 10 percent of the purse, he could have spent New Year's Eve counting his 1974 earnings from the more than $4 million.

Most money won in a year, jockey: $4,231,441, Laffit Pincay Jr., 1974

Zander Hollander, a sportswriter on the late *New York World-Telegram,* wrote *Yankee Batboy,* was co-author of *The Sports Nostalgia Quiz Book* and *The Home Run Story,* and has edited numerous books, including *The Complete Encyclopedia of Ice Hockey* and *The Modern Encyclopedia of Basketball.*

David Schulz is co-author of *The Sports Nostálgia Quiz Book,* was senior editor and writer on the twenty volume series *The Ocean World of Jacques Costeau,* and contributing editor to *The Modern Encyclopedia of Basketball* and other sports publications. He wrote sports for Associated Press and was a staffer on *The Morning Telegraph.*

Other SIGNET Books You'll Enjoy